TOUCHSTONE

ECONOMICS
in Plain English

**ALL YOU NEED TO KNOW ABOUT ECONOMICS
—IN LANGUAGE ANYONE CAN UNDERSTAND**

Leonard Silk

A TOUCHSTONE BOOK
Published by Simon and Schuster
New York

A Touchstone Book
Published by Simon and Schuster
A Division of Gulf & Western Corporation
Simon & Schuster Building
Rockefeller Center
1230 Avenue of the Americas
New York, New York 10020
TOUCHSTONE and colophon are trademarks
of Simon & Schuster

Manufactured in the United States of America

1 2 3 4 5 6 7 8 9 10
2 3 4 5 6 7 8 9 10 11 Pbk.

Library of Congress Cataloging in Publication Data
Silk, Leonard Solomon, date.
  Economics in plain English.
  (A Touchstone book)
  Bibliography: p.
  Includes index.
  1. Economics.   I. Title.
HB171.S5625   1979 330   79-13171

ISBN 0-671-22604-5
ISBN 0-671-25051-5 Pbk.

To my sisters—Ada, Doris and Frimi

Contents

ECONOMICS
in Plain English

Preface

This book is based on the proposition that every major idea of economics can be simply expressed. Helping you to understand economics and to put it to work in your own best interests is the purpose of this book.

The abstract language and theories of economics have made many a person feel that this subject is just too difficult and too dull to be worth the effort. Alas, this is true for most laymen of a great deal of the economic literature, as it is of the literature of physical sciences and social sciences.

But the importance of economics to people in their daily lives—in the "ordinary business of life," as Alfred Marshall put it—is too great for economics to be brushed aside as either irrelevant or too difficult. Economics does not have to be dull. Applied to the real problems of your life, and everyone else's life, it can be compelling, exciting . . . and useful.

Is Economics Necessary?

Unfortunately, yes.

It is true that the ascent of man, as J. Bronowski has shown, proceeded nicely for several million years without the assistance of economics. But the double revolutions of capitalism and industrialism, bringing huge numbers of producers and consumers together in a more or less integrated economic system, stirred up curiosity about how the economic system achieved its purposes though uncontrolled and unguided by a central intelligence.

The classical economists, Adam Smith and his followers, were impressed with how beautifully the system worked, guided, as it were, only by the invisible hand of God. "Leave it alone and all will be well" was the reverent message.

But later on, when the system showed signs of breaking

down from massive upheavals of boom, inflation, depression and unemployment, various Mr. Fixits appeared. The greatest of these in the nineteenth century was Karl Marx, who said that the only way to cure the instability of the admittedly rapidly expanding capitalist system—and get rid of its beastly injustice to the poor—was to wipe out private ownership of capital, on which the power of the new ruling class, the bourgeoisie, was founded. The working class, which created all value and suffered misery for its pains under the existing capitalist system, said Marx, should collectively manage its own affairs.

For years academic economists—there were scarcely any others—stuck with Smith, rejecting Marx as the messenger of social upheaval, political dictatorship and economic inefficiency. The Russian Revolution was waged in the name of Marx, but the Revolution's bitter fruits only confirmed the faith of bourgeois economists in *laissez faire*.

With the Great Depression of the 1930's, however, leave-it-alone economics went through its own internal intellectual revolution, with John Maynard Keynes acting as captain.

Capitalism, it appeared, had broken down, as Marx had warned it would. Keynes said it could be saved by having government interfere in the system in a limited way, by increasing the monetary demand for goods and services enough to get rid of unemployment. This Keynesian approach worked well enough to cure the Great Depression—with the help of massive government spending required to wage World War II.

Alas, however, this approach to economic stability bred chronic inflation. And fighting inflation merely by having government reduce total demand bred recession and unemployment. This is where we are now, plagued by unemployment or inflation or both at the same time.

In quest of a solution, economists say economics is the only wheel in town. Noneconomists say, "Some wheel!" but they flock to hear economists analyze, prescribe, and preach.

Society's misery is the economists' good fortune. Businessmen employ economists in large numbers or consult them at high fees, believing that their cracked crystal balls are better than none at all. The press pursues the best-known seers. While many laymen may be annoyed by economists, other social scientists *hate* them—for their fame, Nobel Prizes, and ready access to political power.

Yet anyone who meddles in economic issues becomes an economist of sorts. A generation ago, James Thurber and E. B. White asked, "Is sex necessary?" Masters and Johnson have answered, "Nonsex is a form of sex." Noneconomics is a form of economics. Economics is necessary.

And it can even be engrossing. A belief persists among noneconomists that economics is about dreary abstractions, and that man himself enters economics only as an abstraction, a profit-maximizing or welfare-maximizing construct known as Economic Man. To some degree the complaint is historically justified. But nowadays economists are searching for a new model of man, one fully endowed with humanity.

As such a model, they might consider Leibel Bistritzky, who operates a kosher grocery at 27½ Essex Street on the lower East Side of Manhattan. Mr. Bistritzky asks his customers to leave his grocery every afternoon at four o'clock so that *mincha*—afternoon prayers—can be held in the store for Orthodox Jews who work in the neighborhood. A reporter for *The New Yorker* quoted one of Mr. Bistritzky's neighbors

17

as saying, "He's a man with a soul. Nobody else would do it—close a store when he has twenty customers."[1]

Does economics need Bistritzky? Or is he too complicated? Earlier economists recognized well enough that Economic Man was an abstraction but held that he was a "rational" model that enabled economics to focus on certain aspects of people's behavior aimed at advancing their material interests. The power and pervasiveness of *self-interest* was held to be the kind of brilliant simplification that all sciences search for, like Darwin's concept of natural selection or Newton's concept of gravity.

Alfred Marshall, the great British economist, whose *Principles of Economics*[2] is considered the fairest, final flower of classic economic theory, offered this defense of Economic Man: "Religious motives are more intense than economic, but their direct action seldom extends over so large a part of life. For the business by which a person earns his livelihood generally fills his thoughts during by far the greater part of those hours when his mind is at its best; during them his character is being formed by the way in which he uses his faculties in his work, by the thoughts and the feelings which it suggests, and by his relations to his associates in work, his employers or his employees." So Marshall humbly defined economics as "the study of mankind in the ordinary business of life."

But does Economic Man, that profit maximizer, provide a realistic model of human behavior, even in the ordinary business of life? Does a corporate manager, for instance, put the profits of his corporation or the payout of dividends to stockholders ahead of his own quest for income, wealth, status, and perquisites?

Does a worker really put maximizing his wages above

maintaining solidarity with his fellow union members—whether out of feelings of a community of interests, worry about job security or simply from laziness, inertia, and boredom with work?

Do consumers, confronted with inflation, rush to buy more before prices go up—or do they suffer psychological stress that causes them to cut their spending and increase their saving when prices are climbing?

Harvey Leibenstein, an economics professor at Harvard, contends that answering such questions realistically calls for a drastic overhaul of existing economic theory. He offers instead what he calls "selective rationality" as the basic psychological concept to account for people's economic behavior.[3] The theory of selective rationality implies that people make economic decisions on the basis of a compromise between the way they would like to *see* themselves behave and the way they would *wish* to behave in the absence of any constraints.

The way people would like to "see themselves behave," according to this view, is determined by social standards—or, in Freudian terms, by the individual's superego.

But the way they would "wish to behave in the absence of any constraints" is determined by their inner drives or appetites for food, sex, money, power, or other forms of self-gratification—which Freud labeled the id.

A great deal of conventional economic theory has to be reworked once we accept a richer and more realistic model of man and accept the prime movers of economics as real people, with inner conflicts and confusions, appetites and egos, ids and superegos—their conflicting selfishness and worry about social standards and ethics.

Do people always go after the most they can get, or are

they sometimes satisfied with enough? Professor Herbert Simon of Carnegie-Mellon University offers strong evidence that business managers often settle for "enough"—they behave as profit "satisficers," not profit maximizers. They compromise among social pressures, labor demands, stockholder pressures, their own personal goals, and the need to earn enough money for the firm to ensure its survival and, if possible, its growth.

Conventional economic theory focuses on a business as though it were an entity with a single mind directing it toward a well-defined objective. But there is no collective corporate mind. In focusing on the motivations and conflicts among and within individuals, we come closer to understanding the seeming irrationality of much corporate behavior—as when a valuable manager is dismissed by a chairman whom he made feel uncomfortable or an unprofitable acquisition is pushed through to satisfy an executive's ego or personal interest.

Conventional theory assumes an identity of interests between the principals and agents of a business firm. But, as many cases of bribery and corruption have demonstrated, agents and principals may have different interests. Seemingly stupid or irrational behavior for Gulf Oil or Lockheed Aircraft may have been perfectly rational for Agent X or Principal Y.

Conventional economists may accuse consumers of behaving "irrationally"—for instance, by saving more and spending less in a time of inflation. But once the simplistic assumption of conventional economic theory is dropped (that a rational person should buy more before prices go higher) consumer decisions *not* to buy in a time of inflation may be revealed as quite rational or at least understandable. Professor George

Katona of the University of Michigan explains: "The better off people feel, the more they spend, and the worse off they feel, the less they spend. Inflation makes people feel worse off; when prices increase, living standards worsen, or improve to a lesser extent than a person feels entitled to, in view of his rising income."[4]

People commonly attribute their increases in income to their own efforts, and not to inflation, so they resent the inflation and feel cheated by it even when their own wages or salaries have risen faster than the general price level. They react by spending less.

Inflation also creates uncertainty—an upsetting state of mind that increases people's tendency to save. They often feel that they will need more money in the future to pay for necessities and ought not to spend money now for luxuries or "discretionary" items that they can do without.

Inflation may also cause people to tighten up on current spending as they think of the future needs of their children —for instance, for money to pay the rising costs of a college education. The superego may triumph over the id, though sometimes the id wins out. *Conflict* is the constant.

The Uses of Rationality

But the need for economic rationality in order to comprehend and resolve conflicts and problems is far from dead. With respect to inflation, for instance, businessmen appear to behave more as conventional economic theory assumes they should, buying more when prices are expected to rise, buying less when prices are expected to fall. In recent years when inflation soared—and consumers cut their spending

21

and raised their savings rate—business firms increased their inventories in anticipation of rising prices and cut their inventories when prices began to drop.

The pressures of the market often compel the businessman to behave "rationally." To increase his profits, he seeks to determine just what the market for his products will be, whether he should maintain his prices, increase or reduce them, increase or reduce his advertising expenditures, add to or reduce his sales staff.

He must seek to reduce his costs of doing business to meet the pressures of competition from other businesses. He must decide whether to buy new machinery to increase the productivity of his plant; seek to substitute less expensive materials for more expensive ones; try to employ people who will produce enough to cover their cost—and possibly add to profits.

The businessman must be alert to new industrial developments that may create new opportunities for him, and when such developments arise, he must decide whether to switch to different types of production or try to develop new products through research. He must determine whether he has enough productive capacity to meet the demand for his products, whether he has enough warehouse space for his goods, and whether he has sufficient distribution established for getting his goods to possible buyers. He must study his financial situation continuously.

Determining the answers to all these questions involves collecting information, analyzing economic and financial data, making rational business decisions, and applying his hunches about the prospects of particular actions. The businessman lives in a world that cannot be perfectly measured, and he must have the courage to rely on his instincts; but clear economic information and analysis can undoubtedly help him make better business decisions and reduce the amount of uncertainty that he faces, and thus help his business prosper.

So rationality lives—and businessmen must go on making the fine calculations between more and less. But they have grown increasingly subject to the constraints of government and civic groups, and perhaps to the inner pressures of social standards—whether these are called superego, after Freud, or simply conscience, that "still, small voice that says you might get caught."

Within the same constrained environment, individuals also strive to make rational spending decisions, a little more on this, and a little less on that—more on insulation, less on heat; more on vegetables, less on meat; more on tomato juice, less on vodka (or vice versa)—as they try to increase their personal satisfactions.

So, too, with nations. The power to make rational economic decisions affects the ability of nations to deal with their domestic and international problems, from unemployment to war, and hence affects their growth or decline.

Economic rationality is not the enemy of humanity but its friend.

CHAPTER TWO
Why Economists Disagree

Economists try to do what all scientists do—observe certain aspects of the natural or social world, gather data to measure those aspects, construct theories to explain the data, and test the theories against reality to validate or invalidate them. On the whole, however, economists do a weak job at all this. They commonly spend vast amounts of time observing each other's articles rather than reality. Their data are poor, and they devote little time to improving them. Their theories are rigid and mechanistic. And they rarely discard them unless some academic or government position is at stake.

Is Economics a Science?

Yet the weakness of economics as a science isn't entirely the fault of the economists. The reality they are trying to analyze and predict doesn't lend itself to orderly and closed systems of analysis like, say, physics. The physicist can exclude "outside" disturbances, such as national elections or wars, from the particular system of atoms he is studying. The economist can't really exclude anything that affects the economic system. His system is "open"—open to the storms of political, social, technological, psychological, and even climatic change. Not being able to predict all such changes, his powers to forecast the economy are weak. His very perception of reality is weak; his seemingly hard and precise numbers are soft, synthetic, inaccurate reflections of underlying events and moods and tendencies. One worthwhile reform of economic statistics might be to outlaw the decimal point.

The problem of achieving scientific objectivity is worsened for the economist by his conscious or unconscious political and social biases and values. Is he a Republican or a Democrat, a disciple of Smith or Marx or Jesus or Ayn Rand? Does he identify with the rich, the poor or the middle class? Is he an elitist or a populist?

Does he believe that political freedom depends on preserving economic freedom and that economic freedom is achievable only under capitalism? Or does he believe that the great corporations of mature capitalist societies tend to abridge both political and economic freedom?

Does he conceive of society as a continuous struggle among classes, with the state the instrument of the dominant class, or does he see democratic society as one in which the state can and often does serve some general public interest?

All such questions are not just scientific; they are political, philosophical, and ethical questions as well.

It would help if economists made their political and social values explicit, rather than pretending to a spurious scientism. Unfortunately, concealed biases and interested political or economic motives commonly corrupt both economic analysis and policy.

Is Economics Propaganda?

The struggle for an objective economics has been going on for a long time. Back in the days before Adam Smith, in the sixteenth, seventeenth, and eighteenth centuries, the first economists were businessmen—international traders and merchants, known as "mercantilists" in the economic literature. Their economics was a form of special pleading for their own interests; they identified those interests passionately with those of the nation—as businessmen have tended to do ever since. "What's good for the nation is good for General Motors, and vice versa," said "Engine Charlie" Wilson. In 1621, Thomas Mun, a manager of the East India Company, put the thought somewhat differently: "The nation is like a big family."

What was good for one, said the mercantilists, was good for all. As it was good for a merchant to amass riches, so was it for the nation. So the nation should save more than it spent, sell more than it bought. If it did so, gold would flow in to balance the nation's accounts. A "favorable" (surplus) balance of trade was the road to wealth for the nation.

England and other nations, pursuing the mercantilist philosophy, tried to acquire wealth by keeping out foreign goods—by taxing imports heavily and granting monopolies to their own ships. The net effect of these efforts on every nation's part to run a surplus (which is obviously impossible for all) was to *diminish* trade and make individual nations poorer not richer.

Adam Smith's Beneficent System of the World

Modern economics was born in Adam Smith's effort to refute the mercantilists. He built a system of thought to demonstrate how a nation's interests—and all nations' interests— would best be served by the free flow of trade within an interdependent world economic system, whether an individual company's or industry's immediate interests were hurt or not.

Unlike the mercantilists, Smith was no businessman but an academic, a professor of moral philosophy at the University of Edinburgh. Like many of his contemporaries, Smith worked under the influence of two great Englishmen who had preceded him by a generation—Sir Isaac Newton, the physicist, and John Locke, the philosopher.

Newton's *Principia Mathematica* had described the physical universe as a precise machine, powered by a few simple forces; after Newton, scholars sought to find the same kind of order in human beings and in human society. The human body, with its delicate network of nerves, muscles, glands, organs, worked marvelously well without apparent human will or direction. Societies of animals and insects constituted organic systems. Could not human society be the same? A Scottish philosopher, Thomas Reid, compared human society to a bee colony. While constructing a honeycomb of perfect hexagons, bees did not first set out to solve the geometry of the hive; each bee built without knowing what he was doing in relation to all other bees. Similarly, Reid argued, man did not know the ultimate purposes of his actions. He was guided by immediate impulses and emotions which somehow fit into a large plan.

Another philosopher, Bernard de Mandeville, shocked the respectable Adam Smith by arguing that private vices might be public virtues. Mandeville's didactic poem "The Fable of the Bees or Private Vices, Public Benefits" sought to show that social benefits might flow from individual actions that might be regarded as morally objectionable; thus he praised spending (which created work for others) and deplored saving (which dried up trade). Mandeville even celebrated the social utility of sexual passion, whatever the purposes of the lovers; "I much question whether the civilized pair, in the most chaste of their embraces, ever acted from the care of their species, as an active principle." This may have disturbed the respectable Smith, but it was close to his own ideas. In *The Theory of Moral Sentiments,* which preceded his famous *Wealth of Nations* by seventeen years, Smith wrote that we control ourselves and feel sympathy for others not out of any overwhelming love of mankind, but rather to satisfy our own most important desires—to be loved and to be cared for. The result is that, in trying to gratify ourselves, we individuals unwittingly benefit society.

Smith blended this rather weak defense of self-interest with the strong ideas of Locke on the natural rights of man. Government ruled only by the consent of the governed, and its power must be carefully limited to serving the public interest. It was the individual who really mattered; the Lockean idea that every person had an inherent right to "life, liberty, and the pursuit of happiness"—as Thomas Jefferson phrased the principle—lay at the heart of both the American political revolution and Smith's economic revolution. Smith's great work of 1776—its full title was *An Inquiry into the Nature and Causes of the Wealth of Nations*[1]—united Newtonian order and Lockean freedom through the concept of an economy built on free markets, free trade, and the pursuit of self-interest. The desire to better our own condition "comes with us from the womb and never leaves us till we go into the grave. . . . It is not from the benevolence of the butcher, the brewer or the baker that we expect our dinner, but from their regard to their own self-interest. We address ourselves, not to their humanity, but to their self-love!"

Yet Smith was no Utopian who believed that the free market provided the solution to every social problem. Often his own best critic, he anticipated many of the injustices of the market that later economists would stress. He warned against capitalist greed and monopolies. He saw the danger that the division of labor in factories would breed intense boredom and what Karl Marx would later call "alienation" among the workers. Smith urged that the growth of industry be paralleled by a growth in education, to keep the worker from being turned into a "brute animal." And he forecast the rise of the bourgeoisie—and the new class antagonisms that would result.

But Smith, child of the Enlightenment, remained an optimist; the Invisible Hand—that most powerful of all his metaphors, and perhaps the strongest in all of economics—would reconcile human conflicts and guide mankind to a happy end, if the state, that monster of the eighteenth century liberals, did not interfere.

Malthus Foresees Continual Human Misery

The Reverend Thomas R. Malthus, who lived on through the industrial revolution well into the nineteenth century, had no faith in Smith's Invisible Hand. More scientist than preacher, though a parson, Malthus looked sharply at his England and saw that much of the population was starving, drinking, or drugging itself to death. Infant mortality rates had never been higher. Gin production and consumption were rising fast. Mothers and young children were being kept at work by being drugged with gallons of opiates. It was Malthus who gave economics the reputation of being "the dismal science," as Thomas Carlyle christened it.

His most famous and debated contributions to the new science were what Kenneth Boulding calls the "Dismal Theorem" and the "Utterly Dismal Theorem." The first states that "if the only ultimate check on the population is misery, then the population will grow until it is miserable enough to stop." The second states: "Any technical improvement will enable population to grow and will soon merely enable *more* people to live in misery than before." An Oxford classmate of Malthus', the poet Samuel Taylor Coleridge, said of the Malthusian principle that population, increasing geometrically, would outrun the means of subsistence, increasing arithmetically: "I solemnly declare that I do not believe that all the heresies and sects and fashions, which the ignorance and the weakness and the wickedness of man have ever given birth to, were altogether so disgraceful to man as a Christian, a philosopher, a statesman or a citizen, as this abominable tenet."

Woe unto Malthus, the bearer of ill tidings! All his life he insisted that his goal was to serve the poor. He could do so only by looking unflinchingly at the facts of life and nature.

Adam Smith and other philosophers of the Enlightenment —said Malthus in the first edition of his *Essay on Population,* published in 1798 when he was thirty—had overlooked the most fundamental facts of human existence—food and sex. While Malthus himself seemed to have been temperate in his love of each, they impressed him more than the formulas for perfection and liberation that his father, a friend of Rousseau's, had raised him on.

Malthus demanded evidence that the problems of scarcity, population growth, poverty, and misery, which had always plagued the world, would not go on doing so: "A writer may tell me that he thinks man will ultimately become an ostrich. I cannot properly contradict him. But before he can expect to bring any reasonable person over to his opinion, he ought to show that the necks of mankind have been gradually elongating, that the lips have grown harder and more prominent and that the legs and feet are daily altering the shape and the hair is beginning to change into stubs of feathers."

The laws of nature were inexorable, said Malthus. Surplus population would die of starvation, violence, war; misery could only be checked by misery—or fear of misery that would give rise to sexual continence. He considered birth control, not very effective in his time, a vice that would encourage promiscuity and make matters worse.

In later editions of his essay on population, Malthus looked for a way out. There was, he granted, a tendency for people who had begun to live better to limit their families, to keep themselves and their children from falling into poverty. If demand could be increased, and production spurred, more people would be employed, their incomes would rise, and they might try to hang on to what they had got.... But Malthus was ahead of his time in arguing that demand could be increased; the age of Keynes was a century away.

Meanwhile, much misery lay ahead. Ireland proved to be a perfect laboratory for the new Malthusian science. At the start of the eighteenth century, two million people had lived in Ireland—fairly miserably—on small grains. Then the potato was introduced; it enabled more people to eat better. Infant mortality fell. By 1845 the Irish population had grown to eight million, and the people were living as poorly on potatoes as their ancestors had on grain. But the total amount of misery, one might say, had increased fourfold.

With the potato famine of 1845, 1846, and 1847 the population of Ireland fell. One million died from starvation and disease and one million emigrated. From eight million in 1845, the population dropped to six million people, most of them living barely above the subsistence level. At this point, the cycle should have started all over again, but this time the Irish chose the second Malthusian option—to check misery with the fear of misery. Late marriage became socially approved. The famine had a lasting effect long after the worst years were past. Ireland's population fell to four million in the mid-1920's and is less than three million today.

But the history of Ireland is not—or not yet—the history of the world. In the poor nations of Asia, Africa, and Latin America, improved nutrition and sanitation have led to a population explosion. Imported foodstuffs and technological advances have barely kept pace; most of the world's population lives close to a Malthusian equilibrium—at the subsistence level. With bad luck and bad harvests, millions will fall below it.

Even in the rich industrial countries, fears are abroad that the Malthusian problem has not vanished. The human population is bound to the earth, with its finite resources. Will the exhaustion of nonrenewable resources eventually do us in? Or can science somehow help us to escape? Will we be compelled to limit population to far lower numbers? Must we, like the Irish, die or emigrate in large numbers—this time to outer space? Parson Malthus' riddle persists.

The solution depends partly on science and technology, but partly also on human desires and the ways human beings organize their societies.

Karl Marx Says Capitalism Is Doomed

The most famous apostate from classical economics, Karl Marx, sought a radical change in the way society was organized. He appreciated the fantastic changes that the capitalist system had brought about—especially its productive power—but nevertheless thought the system was doomed by historical processes. The riddle Marx posed was: "What is to take the place of capitalism once the historical conditions that gave rise to it no longer exist?" That question shook the world—and is still shaking it.

Who was Marx? A lonely German intellectual without an academic post, a convert to Christianity from Judaism, a poor free-lance journalist, a son of the middle class who had married an aristocrat, a passionate revolutionary, he was at the same time a genius, one of those rare figures who transform the world.

A Prussian by birth and education, he left the country when his radical newspaper was shut down by the government. He first settled in Paris, later stayed in Brussels until he was expelled in 1848; he moved briefly back to Germany, to publish a radical newspaper. But in 1848, the year of *The Communist Manifesto*,[2] the French and Prussian police, working together, had Marx expelled from the Continent. He fled to liberal England, the foremost capitalist power of the time.

Soon afterward, a Prussian police spy wrote a description of the slum tenement in Dean Street, Soho, where Marx was living with his wife and three children and their (usually unpaid) servant: "He lives in one of the worst and cheapest neighborhoods in London. He occupies two rooms. There is not one clean or decent piece of furniture in either room, everything is broken, tattered and torn, with thick dust over everything and the greatest untidiness everywhere. In the middle of the parlor there is a large old-fashioned table covered with oilcloth. On it manuscripts, books, and newspapers lie beside the children's toys, bits and pieces from his wife's sewing basket, cups with broken rims, dirty spoons, knives, and forks, lamps, an inkwell, tumblers, some Dutch clay pipes, tobacco ash—all piled up on the same table."

On that very table was born *Das Kapital*—and, in a sense, the Russian and Chinese revolutions. Such is the power of ideas—when joined to the right historical conditions!

Marx used the classical economics against itself. He found nothing divine about the market, no Invisible Hand to guide it toward the greater good of all mankind. A market was simply a social arrangement that men had created— especially those men who stood to profit from the market— and that other men could, and would, in time destroy, when they decided that the market had outlived its usefulness or necessity.

The creed of self-interest, nurtured in the marketplace, could not be regarded as an eternal verity. Marx complained that Smith and his followers had looked only at one historical moment in time and thought they had discovered laws that would be good for all time. It was wrong, he said, for Smith to argue that man always functioned best when he operated according to his self-interest. This may have been true among the class of small capitalists at the end of the eighteenth century, but it certainly was not true in feudal or mercantile states where exchange was dependent on personal loyalties and other noneconomic relationships. Marx admitted that classical economists had gone far in understanding the market, but said that their "laws" of economic behavior were subsumed by a much greater economic relationship, one that existed in every society—that linking the producer to his product. In effect, said Marx, the worker owned what he created—but was cheated of it by "capitalism."

He departed from his predecessors in economics by asking new questions. He wanted to know, not just *how the market worked*, but *how it came to exist in the first place*. He asked, not how to keep the market functioning, but what would replace it.

He had no doubt that the capitalist system was "out of control" and that the market had, like Frankenstein's monster, taken on a life of its own that made prisoners not only of workers but of the entire society. People no longer fulfill themselves in their work, said Marx, but deny their own humanity. They experience misery, not well-being. They do not work to satisfy the need to create, but only to satisfy other needs, to acquire money and possessions.

Thus, said Marx, capitalism changes the whole purpose of community life. In a pre-industrial society, people banded together for protection, to exchange goods, for a whole sphere of communal reasons. But under capitalism, said Marx, the fabric of society is torn to shreds and individuals think only of themselves.

Man's creative impulse, said Marx, is directed by the exigencies of "the system" away from, rather than toward, the community. The individual longs to establish his identity as something more than a statistic, a sale, a unit of labor. But he sees others, in a market society, as competing labor units or competing (and richer) consumers—not as friends but as things.

That was how Marx interpreted Smith's doctrine of self-interest. For Marx, this was not man's natural state but merely a reflection of the poverty of human relationships in a market society.

The result of this radical transformation of society by capitalism, said Marx, was the "fetishism of the commodity." As primitive societies worshipped the sun or the moon, so industrialized man worships the commodity. In Adam Smith's pin factory, each man is at the service of the pin. Even worse was the "fetishism of money" that the market society indulged in. Money conferred a power that was obscene; it induced people to sell themselves—bodies, minds, and principles.

Having voiced his hatred of naked capitalism as he observed it in nineteenth-century England and on the Continent, Marx did not become a reactionary who wanted to turn the clock back to feudalism. He had no illusions about the slavery, serfdom, poverty, misery of the pre-industrial world. Marx was a champion of industrial technology, and felt that it had one overwhelming virtue: it could solve the cardinal economic problem of scarcity.

Scarcity had led to the creation of capitalism; and only by conquering scarcity could a better world be forged. Here Marx, who usually had little use for Malthus, agreed with him that the constraints imposed by natural resources were one of the critical foundations of history. But where Malthus tried to work within those constraints, Marx asserted that they could be broken altogether. This was Marx's great idea: that the means existed for creating a just society in which the struggle for shares could end. As the American socialist Michael Harrington has put it, socialism's "most basic premise is that man's battle with nature has been completely won and that there is therefore more than enough of material goods for everyone."[3]

As he grew older Marx no longer thought that the end of capitalism was nigh; he dropped his apocalyptic warning about its imminent collapse. He realized that he had underestimated the resiliency of the capitalists and their system. Facing the dilemma of whether to make capitalism more humane, and thereby prolong its life, or try to hasten its collapse by encouraging brutal legislation and action, he chose the former. The day when workers could claim their rights and their just estate would come only when the preconditions for a new society existed. Capitalist systems had to grow and mature and age until they were ripe for revolution.

The Russian Revolution, had Marx lived to see it, would have taken him by surprise; it occurred in an embryonic capitalist state, still undelivered from feudalism. So too with the Chinese Revolution.

The harsh suppression of human rights in Communist countries, dominated by a new ruling class, would presumably have appalled and devastated Marx. But it would not have surprised Adam Smith in the least.

The Big Question

Smith, Malthus, and Marx—is there any common thread that binds their economics together? The conflicts in their thought seem fundamental.

Aristotle said one cannot begin the search for knowledge without first accepting that a thing cannot exist and not exist at the same time; otherwise, all philosophy would be non-sensical. In mathematics, one must agree that a number always equals itself; otherwise, any further exploration of numbers would be meaningless.

What in economics must be taken on faith? That people want money? That you get what you pay for? That there is no such thing as a free lunch? That the division of labor increases output? That more output is better than less?

Or do all the axioms change according to whose economics you are talking about?

E. S. Schumacher, the British economist who wrote *Small Is Beautiful*,[4] argues that, unlike the elements in the systems of the natural sciences or mathematics, the axioms in an economic system can be devised by the actors themselves. By this he does not mean that they can decide whether or not to believe in the laws of supply and demand or diminishing returns, both of which have massive empirical support; rather, he contends, human beings can control what might be called the metaphysical question of economics—

the question that must be answered before any data are collected, before any laws theorized. "What does it mean for something to be economical?" might be called the meta-question of economics.

Two hundred years ago, Adam Smith proposed a meta-answer that has never been seriously challenged: Economics is about wealth creation, and wealth-creating choices are (or should be) made by comparing the amount of time, labor, resources, and capital invested in a project with the return on that investment—and with alternative investments and organizations of production.

In Smith's famous description of a pin factory, it is more "economical" to employ twenty people to make 40,000 pins a day, breaking down the work into many separate tasks, than to employ the same number of workers, each working alone and performing every task—with all of them producing a total of, say, 1,000 pins a day. In Smith's conception, economics is fundamentally a system of thought aimed at telling you how to get more—more pins, more food, more real wealth—out of existing resources.

But this seemingly straightforward approach to the goals of economics, says Schumacher, is not all-comprehending. It leaves out what should be a critical factor: the development of the *worker*.

In Smith's formulation—as in the industrial system—labor is treated as an "input" to production, rather than as an end in itself. But in what Schumacher calls a "Buddhist" economy, guided by the principle that work and leisure are not antagonistic but complementary, with both contributing to the development of mind and body, work might be defined equally in terms of worker and product. The aim of economics would be to enable people to develop their faculties and not just to turn out goods. The goal of economic activity ought not to be to produce as much as possible, but to enable people to gain the most utility and comfort while using up the least amount of resources—especially irreplaceable resources, such as the earth's minerals. The limits to industrial growth might be only decades away; mankind should learn to live within those severe constraints while there is still time.[5]

Many economists find such fears groundless, contending that somehow science and technology will always find a way to expand the world's "finite" resources—or to draw on those of the universe. Nevertheless, the debate over the limits to growth has served to focus attention on the longer-run goals of economics and the ethical issues raised by rapid depletion or pollution of the earth's resources.

The Clash Among Values and Goals

Ethics has been moving up on the agenda of economics as economists become increasingly aware of the necessity of working on the goals of economic policy. Goals are value-laden, rich in ethical content. What are the obligations of a rich society to a poor one? What do we mean by equality? Is it in conflict with efficiency, and if so, how is the conflict to be mediated? A growing number of economists now believe that the economist must concentrate more on such questions—and on the entire process by which goals are set and conflicts resolved among such goals as economic growth, efficiency, equity, security, and stability.

Many economists still consider that goals, in their specific forms, should be taken by the economist as "given"—that is, given by the society in general or by particular policy makers. They have maintained that social and economic goals are subjective, and that economists are no better qualified than anyone else at setting them.

But this self-limiting position has led to a most unhelpful vagueness on the part of economists in an area crucial to the entire realm of economic and social policy. In economics as well as politics, the clash over values and goals is frequently the heart of the problem.

Ethical issues are not absent from the marketplace. A free-market system depends on fairness, trust, and integrity among buyers and sellers. Power is not equally distributed in the marketplace, nor are information and knowledge (which are a form of power); hence the need for ethical standards and rules.

Professor Kenneth Arrow of Harvard, a Nobel laureate in economics, has said that one way our economic system adapts to the unequal distribution of information and knowledge is scarcely mentioned in economists' models—the development of ethical codes by the members of a profession. Every profession owes its function to the inequality of information between the professional and his client. But that is a difficult situation for the market to control with fairness to both professional and client. A patient has little protection against a physician's recommendation of unnecessarily costly treatment other than ethical constraints on the doctor's economic behavior.[6] In every contract, ethical elements enter; no market could function without them. This also holds for economists in the market of ideas.

The deepest divisions among economists stem from their different political and ethical beliefs and from the different economic and social interests they represent, whether consciously or unconsciously. Perhaps the best thing one can do about these sources of difference among economists—and of the resulting confusion to their clients and the general public —is to get the economists' values, politics, and interests out into the open. Meanwhile, let the buyer beware.

CHAPTER THREE
The Language of Economics

In every special field, including sports, crime, and the stock market, words have special meanings for the specialists. Thus, when the economist talks about the "consumption function," he is not necessarily showing off but simply using a term to describe a specific mathematical relationship—the extra spending on consumer goods that results from extra income. There is no other name in the English language for this concept—unless you prefer to call it "the marginal propensity to consume" or "the propensity-to-consume schedule." But it is an important concept. It is crucial to understanding how the economy works and to analyzing the probable effects of a tax cut or a boost in government spending.

This is not to say that, in talking to ordinary citizens, economists have to use such terms as "consumption function." Certainly they should not. In talking to the public, the best economists don't need jargon to say what they mean. They understand their material well enough to put it simply and exactly, in ordinary language. This has some advantages even for the specialists themselves. For jargon can limit, distort or even poison the thinking of those who use it habitually. It can easily degenerate into fakery and display.

The Three Languages of Economics

Paul Samuelson used as the motto for his pathbreaking *Foundations of Economic Analysis* the remark of J. Willard Gibbs, a famous mathematician, that "mathematics is a language."[1] (He said this at a Yale faculty meeting on language requirements.)

Actually, economists have their choice among three languages—mathematics, Economese, and ordinary English (or any other ordinary language).

Every idea can be expressed in all three languages; for instance, here are three ways of expressing our concept of the consumption function:

Mathematics	=	Economese	=	English
$C = f(Y)$		Consumption function		The more we earn, the more we spend; but as our incomes rise, we increase our spending less and less, and increase our saving more and more.
in which C denotes *consumption;* Y, *income;* and f is a symbol for function.		or Marginal propensity to consume		
		or Propensity-to-consume schedule		

Each of the three languages has its strengths and weaknesses. Mathematics, when correctly used, is the most concise and exact. It has the great virtue of being usable not only as a language but also as an instrument for analyzing problems, quantitatively and logically. But, quite apart from its lack of color and resonance, mathematics has the enormous disadvantage as a language of being incomprehensible to most of the general public and, in its higher forms, even to most economists. And mathematics may force the writer into so high a level of abstraction as to lose contact with economic and social reality.

Economese provides tags for concepts and theories that economists find convenient or necessary to use in talking to one another. But Economese is almost as difficult for the public to understand as mathematics (sometimes more so).

Plain English has the advantages not only of intelligibility but, at its best, of cleanliness, resonance, rhythm, and beauty. It is supple—and, for the user, mind-stretching. It forces the economist to reexamine and restate his ideas so that any reasonably intelligent person can understand them. Although it may require more time, effort, and space, the use of plain English can lead to greater accuracy and clarity for the writer as well as the reader; it may provoke fresher and more direct observation of people and events—the true subject matter of economics—rather than an endless scholastic debate about the economic literature.

In a democracy, economists cannot be content to talk only to themselves or to a small elite. They have a critical role to play in helping to bring into being a better-informed citizenry, competent to understand economic issues and act sensibly on important public and private matters.

But the citizenry—or as much of it as possible—has a

corresponding responsibility to try to understand what the economists are saying. The layman can ask the economist to get rid of his jargon, but he cannot ask him to do without his concepts or theories. One cannot conceive of *music* without *rhythm, harmony, counterpoint, notes, scales, keys, chords,* etc. Similarly, one cannot conceive of economics without the concepts of economics. The problem is to make those concepts intelligible.

Why Economic Abstractions Boggle the Mind

Some economic classifications are easy to grasp. What do J. P. Morgan, Henry Ford, Thomas Edison, Robert Vesco, John D. Rockefeller, Bert Lance, Bebe Rebozo, and Rupert Murdoch have in common? Well, they all made money by starting or developing businesses and by taking large financial risks. Their common attribute (with no offense intended to any of them) might be called entrepreneurship, enterprise, risk-taking, innovation—and their style of thought capitalist. But it isn't always this easy to understand an abstract economic classification. Consider, for example:

Oligopoly
An industry—such as automobiles, aluminum, gypsum, electrical generators, detergents, chewing gum, razor blades, rubber, main-frame computers—in which a small number of firms supplies most of the industry's output.
Oligopsony
A market structure—as for sheet steel, rails, primary copper, leaf tobacco, fluid milk, crude petroleum—in which

48

a relatively small number of firms do most of the buying.
Transfer payments
Payments by the government—such as social security benefits, unemployment compensation, and relief checks—for
which no goods are expected in return from the recipients
of the payments. Private firms may also make transfer
payments, such as corporate gifts to colleges, hospitals or
other nonprofit institutions.

Most laymen have trouble with the abstractions and gen-
eralizations of economics because their meanings are not
clear on first sight, the terms are not defined, and the economist often seems to prefer obscurity. There is no reason why
an economist who doesn't want to interrupt the flow of his
thought to give a full definition of "transfer payments" cannot at least say, ". . . social security and other transfer payments," with a quick gain in intelligibility to the reader.

Many economists are addicted to jawbreakers and mind-
bogglers, such as *X-inefficiency, short-term profit maximi-
zation, equi-productive effort points, residual impactees,
flat-top utility-effort functions, socioeconomic influence contracts, empathy utility, separability hypotheses, carte-blanche
reference variables,* etc. Some economists write English as
though they were translating from nineteenth-century German; they love to string nouns together. Walter Salant of
the Brookings Institution has a particular antipathy toward
nouns used to modify nouns to modify other nouns. When
he began to run up against five-noun terms, such as *terminal
traffic control program category,* Salant launched a campaign
for a mandatory two-noun limit on economists.[2]
Communication between the economist and the layman

sometimes breaks down because words in Economese look as though they are words in standard English; the Economese word often stands for a mathematical model or economic theory which the economist knows but the layman does not.

Take the word "demand," as in the phrase "demand for oil." To the layman, this looks like an ordinary English word that refers to how much of a product the public wants to buy. But to the economist, the word "demand" represents a mathematical model, a demand schedule showing the different quantities of oil that the public would be willing to purchase *at various prices*. So the layman may think of demand as a point, and the economist thinks of it as a curve. Who is right, layman or specialist, working stiff or intellectual, citizen or elitist, is not a matter of taste, style, or opinion. The economist conceptualizes and defines demand as a curve because that concept is closer to reality and more useful in analysis. But, knowing that the layman may be thinking of demand as a point, the economist should promptly clarify his use of the term "demand" to increase public understanding. Seeing demand as a curve, as a function of price, is crucial, for example, to the development of national energy policy and public support of a policy to conserve fuel.

The concept of demand includes other concepts, such as:

Price elasticity of demand
    The degree of responsiveness of the demand for a good (such as oil) to changes in its price.
Income elasticity of demand
    The degree of responsiveness of the demand for a good to changes in the income of consumers.

Economic terms denoting economic theories sometimes bear the name of the economist credited with inventing the theory. This is a nice way for an economist to achieve immortality. Thus we have:

Pareto-optimality
Named for Vilfredo Pareto. A state of the economy from which no possible movement could be made that would make *everyone* better off. (Things are Pareto-optimal when improving my lot must worsen yours.)

Gresham's Law
Named for Sir Thomas Gresham. Bad money drives out good. (Who would want to pay his debts with good money if he could settle them legally with bad money?)

Giffen's Paradox
Named for Sir Robert Giffen. When prices of inferior (that is, lower quality) goods rise, people will buy more of them. (Rising prices of certain "inferior" goods, such as potatoes, cut into people's income so much that they buy more of the inferior goods to stay alive. This happened during the potato famine in Ireland in 1845.)

Slutsky's Proposition
Named for E. Slutsky. This indecent-sounding proposition holds that the moving average of a random series oscillates.

Indeed, Slutsky's Proposition serves to indicate why it is so easy for economists to find business cycles in any complex mass of data over periods of time. So we have Kitchin cycles (40 months long), Juglar cycles (1 Juglar equals 3 Kitchins), Kondratieff cycles (18 Kitchins equal 1 Kondratieff—hence the K cycle is said to occur every 50 to 60 years).

In a celebrated sentence in his witty presidential address to the American Economic Association in 1961, Samuelson spoke of his esoteric work on "substitutability relations in Minkowski-Ricardo-Leontief-Metzler matrices of Mosak-Hicks type." Economists think it is classy to use the names of other economists adjectivally—as in Keynesian, Pigouvian, Marshallian, Ricardian, Walrasian, Paretian, etc. Latin phrases also lend a touch of class—especially *ceteris paribus* ("other conditions being equal") and *pari passu* ("with equal progress"), that is, when one variable changes simultaneously and equally with another.

The Art of Euphemism

Economese is sometimes productive of delightful euphemisms, some of which have done their bit to dull or mask human misery. Thus, economic *panic* gave way to *depression* and, when depression became too painful, to *recession*.

Similarly, *poor* and *backward countries* gradually evolved into *underdeveloped countries*, which then became *less developed countries* (LDC's), and finally emerged as proud *developing countries*. On the other hand, *rich countries* became *developed countries*, and—in the current ideological climate at the United Nations—may eventually wind up as *overdeveloped countries* (OC's).

An economist might have written:

> Objective consideration of contemporary phenomena compels the conclusion that success or failure in competitive activities exhibits no tendency to be commensurate with innate capacity, but that a considerable

52

element of the unpredictable must inevitably be taken into account.[3]

Actually, however, that sentence is a translation by George Orwell of the verse from Ecclesiastes that goes:

> I returned, and saw under the sun, that the race is not to the swift, nor the battle to the strong, neither yet riches to men of understanding, nor yet favor to men of skill; but time and chance happeneth to them all.

The Concepts Behind the Jargon

The job of translating genuine, original Economese into plain English is far more difficult. How would you like to try your hand at translating the following two passages:

> Since regulatory constraints are often inequalities, there are ranges of values for the regulatory parameters such that regulation, for the time being, has no effect on the behavior of the firm. The profit-permissibility function will then coincide with the profit-possibility function without regulation close to the latter's maximum, although elsewhere the two may diverge.[4]

And here is a carefully constructed sentence concerning factors involved in economic growth:

> If we postulate a well-behaved CES production function which is first degree homogeneous in the arguments labor, L, and the simple aggregate of all land and conventional reproducible capital, Kt, it be-

comes necessary to accept one of the two following conditions as true: either (1) the constant elasticity of substitution between labor and all capital exceeded unity, so that over the course of the century the share of the factor that had increased in relative abundance was *enlarged,* or (2) the elasticity of substitution was less than unity but capital-deepening technological change lowered the ratio of capital to labor when both are measured in efficiency units, rendering capital services the increasingly scarce input reckoned on an efficiency basis.[5]

The problem for the ordinary reader in understanding such passages is not that their authors are trying to show off nor that they are trying to soften or obscure their meaning. No, the real problem is that the concepts the economists are using—the concepts that lie behind the words—are unknown to the general reader, so the economist might as well be writing in Sanskrit or Urdu.

You cannot understand Economese—or, what is much more important, economics—without learning its underlying concepts.

CHAPTER FOUR
Key Concepts

Can the key concepts of economics be simply stated? Let's try.

RESOURCES: Anything that can be employed to produce economic goods or provide services—such as arable land, oil, natural gas, minerals, forests, waterfalls and all other kinds of natural resources; human beings with their various strengths, skills, talents, and brains; plant, equipment, dams, generators, telephone systems, airports, airplanes, and all other forms of capital goods; mathematics, logic, science, technology, and other forms of human knowledge, some of which are embodied in machines, some in the minds of people, and some stored in libraries, computers, etc.

Resources are *necessarily* used in the production of goods

—or, as economists love to say in one of their hoariest jokes, "There is no such thing as a free lunch," or TINSTAAFL. Of course, strictly speaking, there *is* such a thing as a free lunch —not just manna from heaven, but mother's milk, apples that fall on your head, berries beside the road, plankton (if you happen to be a whale), the pleasures of the sun in the morning and the moon at night, running brooks, fresh breezes, the oceans, the atmosphere, love. Some of these free goods become economic goods as civilization advances. But it is well to remember that both free goods and economic goods are capable of satisfying . . .

HUMAN WANTS: These are both physical and psychic, and usually both together. Food satisfies a physical want, but caviar at $500 a pound obviously does a lot more than supply calories; so do our clothes, houses, cars, furniture, not to mention our books, films, sessions with psychoanalysts, lawyers, tennis coaches. Even doing nothing—leisure—fulfils a psychic want. Doing nothing may become the greatest aspiration of some people, those who aspire to the leisure class.

SCARCITY: The gap between human wants and the means of satisfying them.

The age of scarcity is not ending, as John Kenneth Galbraith suggested two decades ago in *The Affluent Society*. On the contrary, because of rapid economic growth and the drain on nonrenewable natural resources, scarcity may be increasing. To be sure, one might end scarcity by reducing human wants rather than by trying endlessly to increase output. But, thrusting aside the "limits to growth" issue, the economist sees scarcity around him everywhere, every day, in little things as well as big—in the strain on family budgets and government budgets, in people's conflicting wants for more income and less work.

Scarcity is really what economics is all about. Scarcity and choice.

CHOICE: To economize is to choose. Each individual must choose how best to satisfy his wants by allocating his limited time and energy to different uses and by distributing his income among the goods and services he wants to buy.

Each business organization must choose how to allocate its limited capital, labor, natural resources, management, and knowledge to achieve its objectives, including profits, growth, and the satisfying of public and governmental pressures.

Each nation must decide how limited resources can best be used to satisfy both the present and future needs and desires of its people—or of their leaders (not necessarily the same needs and desires). At a high level of generality, each nation can be said to have the same problems of deciding what goods to produce, how to produce them, who shall get them, and how much production and employment there will be both now and in the future.

Whether the problem of choice confronts the individual, a business organization or a nation, solving the problem will involve some cost.

OPPORTUNITY COST: What you give up, in making one thing, by not making something else.

Since resources (with the sole exception of knowledge in certain forms) are finite and scarce, you can ordinarily satisfy one want only by not satisfying another want. If you use a field to grow oats, you can't use it at the same time to grow beans. If you use a day to produce thing A, you can't use it to make thing B. Time itself is limited. The opportunity cost of devoting a given amount of resources to national defense, for example, is not devoting those resources to social welfare—or vice versa. Thus, societies must make "trade-offs"—between guns and butter, energy and the environment, production of more goods versus more leisure, and so on, whenever resources are limited. So must individuals and businesses.

COST-BENEFIT ANALYSIS: An evaluation of what you spend or sacrifice in relation to what you get. This should be the basis on which you make choices and trade-offs.

If benefits exceed costs, a particular use of resources makes sense, though not as much sense as some other use where the benefits would exceed the costs by even more. This principle holds for all economic decisions, whoever makes them and however the decisions are made, whether by a single decision maker or by the interaction of many decision makers in a market.

MARGINALISM AND EQUILIBRIUM: Most economic decisions are about a bit more of this or a bit less of that; we choose "at the margin." Consumers don't decide to give up meat altogether, if meat prices go up, but to buy a bit less of it, and substitute a bit more fish for meat. A businessman doesn't decide to get rid of all his workers if wages go up more than productivity, but he may decide to trim his work force and substitute machinery for workers in his effort to maintain or increase his profits. And, within a nation or the world economy, shifts go on all the time at the margin, with some workers and producers shifting from one line of production to another, with one nation expanding its output of electronics and cutting its output of textiles, and another exporting more of its foodstuffs and importing more of its oil.

All these shifts at the margin are conceived by economists as tending toward a state of "equilibrium," in which the consumer is satisfied with his pattern of consumption and sees no advantage in further change, the businessman has done what he could in response to higher wages or other costs and pressures, and the nations have ceased sorting out their division of labor and are ready to settle for the existing market structure. Of course, no such state of general equilibrium exists or has ever existed; life is change, imbalance, readjustment. Nevertheless, the concept of equilibrium has some usefulness for the economist in indicating the direction of change, and how the current problems of choice may be resolved before new disturbances occur.

ECONOMIC SYSTEM: The setup in any nation that determines how resources will be used; what goods and what services will be produced; who will get them, and whether and how much the economy's capability of producing goods will grow.

A "command" system is one in which the government makes all those major decisions. A "market" system is one in which many firms and individuals, casting their "dollar votes" in the marketplace and interacting with each other, determine the answers. "Mixed" economic systems contain both "command" and "market" elements. Democratic socialism is such a mixture, with emphasis on public goods and social control of business. Communism is basically a command system, capitalism basically a market system, but in all advanced industrial societies (such as the Soviet Union and the United States) each system contains an admixture of the other. Purists within each system—hard-line Stalinists in the Soviet Union, libertarians in the United States—would like, to the extent possible, to get rid of the disparate elements of the other system. Purists often feel highly emotional or even religious about expelling what they regard as the alien "command" or "market," capitalist or socialist elements, as the case may be.

THE PROFIT SYSTEM: Those who think they understand it are constantly berating those who they think don't.

Profits are essential to capitalism. No business can survive without some. But that is not to say that any given level of profits is economically necessary or desirable. Competition is supposed to regulate the rate of profit of any firm or industry. Profits may be very high for some industry for a period of time because of growing demand or technological breakthroughs, and the high profits are supposed to attract new resources to expand production in that industry. But profits in that industry may stay high because of the existence of monopoly or oligopoly and the difficulty of entry by new firms.

Profits help provide capital for business investment in plant and equipment. Businessmen can also raise funds by borrowing at banks and from other savers through new stock or bond issues, but it helps firms to have some profits to show if they ever expect to repeat the process of borrowing.

In 1977 corporate profits after taxes amounted to 6.7 percent of national income—much less than most people believe. Several polls have found that the public generally thinks that corporate profits amount to one-third or more of national income.

ECONOMIC INCENTIVES: Businessmen regard profits as the elixir of life and are inclined to treat them reverently. They grow furious with those whom they accuse of regarding profits as a dirty word. Profits, they say, are the incentive for creativity and efficiency. Profits are the preserver of liberty. Lemuel Boulware, a retired vice-president of General Electric Company and a titan of tough bargaining with labor unions, said, "Profit, property, and freedom are inseparable. . . . Profit benefits the nonowners much more than it does the owners of a business. Profit is even the poor man's best friend. It is the greatest engine of human betterment ever devised by man."

But non-true believers ask whether greater corporate profits and social welfare necessarily coincide. If particular companies' pursuit of greater profits means the rapid exhaustion of a scarce resource (such as soil or minerals), society may suffer, they say. Similarly, they add, the search for greater profits may influence foreign policy in dangerous or wasteful ways (as by maximizing arms sales to the Middle East or swelling the production of military hardware for national use or storage for future use).

In short, the cost-benefit ratio of individual firms, as measured by profits, does not necessarily correspond to the cost-benefit ratios for the nation or the world as a whole. The sum of optimal, profit-maximizing decisions by firms may or may not be the best decision for the society as a whole.

The toughest part of national and global decision making is measuring true costs and benefits; the same resources can be shifted to many different uses, and some costs (like that of pollution) are hard to calculate. It is also difficult to measure potential benefits, such as those of clean air, better-educated minds, a richer cultural scene or peace itself (within cities or between nations).

Practically speaking, even if one has a good idea of the national or global cost-benefit ratios and seeks to shift resources to better uses, it may be hard to get the people who control those resources to shift them or allow them to be shifted—because of habits or vested interests. A particular company or region doesn't always want to give up its defense orders; a labor union doesn't want to see jobs moved to another region or country where the benefits might be larger for the society as a whole, but not for the individual union and its members.

Those who habitually praise the free-enterprise, profit, or market system don't like to submit to the discipline of the market when it affects their own interests adversely, even if only in the short run.

MARKETS: Minisystems (or microsystems—their study is called microeconomics) in which particular goods and services are exchanged at a price, with the traders free to sell or not sell what they have for what they want.

Communist systems have markets (such as the markets for vodka or mandolins or underwear, as well as black or illegal markets) but the state plans and coordinates the (legal) markets. Capitalist systems are coordinated mainly by changing prices, costs, and profits.

INTERDEPENDENCE: In capitalist systems, all markets are interdependent, with money, goods, and services flowing from market to market, from consumers to producers to workers, and so on, around and around in a "circular" way. Money flows one way and goods and services flow the other, in an ever-continuing series of voluntary exchanges. The exchanges are voluntary because each party sees an advantage to himself or herself in the trade; thus, exchange is not what mathematicians call a zero-sum game (1 gainer + 1 loser = 0) but a positive-sum game in which both buyer and seller consider themselves winners—although one may win more than the other. But if any rational buyer or seller considers himself a net loser by an exchange, the exchange will not take place. Of course, people can be gypped—but they do not know that at the time they make the deal, or they will not make it. And some people may regret having to sell something they own at a loss or buy something at a price far above what they had intended; but if they go ahead, it is presumably because it would cost them even more if they did not.

SPECIALIZATION, COMPARATIVE ADVANTAGE, AND THE DIVISION OF LABOR: These interlinked ideas explain why voluntary exchange, with benefits to both buyers and sellers, takes place. Specialization—the concentration of a producer (individual, business, or nation) on a narrower range of production than all the things it consumes—occurs because it results in greater efficiency; hence, the same resources can be used to produce more goods in total—so that there will be a bigger pie for the different specializers to divide up if they exchange shares of what each has produced with one another.

Each producer has a "comparative advantage" in doing what it does best—and trading for the rest. Just as a highly paid lawyer should not waste his time typing his own briefs (even if he is a better typist than his secretary) or a highly paid doctor should not paint his own house (even if he is a better and faster painter than any he can hire), a nation should concentrate on what it can do best, given its limited resources.

Critics of this argument contend, however, that free trade is a game stacked against labor or against poorer nations. Many labor unions in advanced countries claim that free trade undermines wage standards and shifts jobs to low-wage countries; they reject the counterargument of free-trade advocates that a rise in total productivity and output will increase the workers' share of a bigger pie, insisting that many workers thrown out of their old jobs cannot or will not move to the industries with "comparative advantage." Those who recognize that there is reality to this claim often propose that government should help the immediate sufferers from free trade to "adjust" by providing subsidies to help them move or to train them for new jobs; in effect, the beneficiaries of free trade ought to "bribe" the victims, and thereby share the benefits with them.

Poor countries also contend that rich, industrial countries have profited unduly and unfairly from free trade. The prices of industrial goods produced by the rich countries, they say, are fixed by powerful industries, while the prices of their own raw materials and minerals are set in highly competitive world markets to their disadvantage. The developing countries assert that their dependence on foreign markets makes their own economic development hazardous: a shift in world market prices can cripple their growth and worsen the misery and hunger of their people, who at best live at the edge of survival. The Malthusian devil is still around, waiting to pick up stragglers, the casualties of changing market conditions.

CHAPTER FIVE
Markets

All economics is divided into two major parts:

MICROECONOMICS (micro = small): The part concerned with the behavior of people and organizations in particular markets; and

MACROECONOMICS (macro = great): The part concerned with the operation of a nation's economy as a whole.

In this chapter we look at microeconomics, the study of particular markets, of which the two most fundamental concepts are *supply* and *demand*.

SUPPLY: The varying amounts of any good that its producers or owners are willing to offer at different prices. As we noted earlier in connection with demand, to the economist supply is not a point (a fixed amount) but a curve that relates quantity to price.

In the case of supply, price and quantity are ordinarily positively correlated; higher prices call forth increased supplies. Some suppliers are "price takers"; they must accept as given the price for their product that is set in the market. Among price takers are the producers of corn and wheat, leather and hides, coal and concrete, alcohol and ammonia, bricks and lime—products which are relatively homogeneous and which have many producers, so that it is easy for customers to substitute the output of one producer for that of another.

But some producers, called "price searchers," have a greater measure of control over a market and look for customers willing to pay the prices they set. Price searchers include local builders or merchants or candy concessionaires in a movie theater who can raise their prices above what outside competitors charge—because their customers find it inconvenient or more costly (including time and transportation costs) to go elsewhere. Some price searchers are big producers, like General Motors or the Aluminum Corporation of America, who are dominant forces in a wide market. And some are producers of highly specialized and desirable goods, such as Gucci shoes, Steuben glass, IBM computers, particular books, films, pharmaceuticals, musical instruments, etc.

Producers of different goods have varying degrees of "elasticity of supply"—the additional quantity they are willing to offer at higher prices. A few products have zero-elasticity of supply; there is only one Hope diamond, and no matter how much anyone is willing to pay, there will never be more than

one Hope diamond—or one Mona Lisa, one Acropolis, one
Marlon Brando. The market can bid the price of them sky-
high without increasing the supply.

But few goods are unique. Some are extremely elastic in
their supply; you can get as many extra paper clips, cans of
dog food, stockings, or copies of a best-selling book as you
like, with little or no increase in price, or even a reduction in
price over time.

Supplies of most goods are more elastic in the long run
than in the short, because it takes time for producers to expand their plant for making more of the product to meet increasing demand. Many goods will fall in price as the
volume of production increases, due to "economies of scale"
resulting from better technology, savings on materials, lower
fixed costs, etc.; this has been the case with radio and TV
sets, ball-point pens, calculators, computers, and chickens.

The general public and most politicians underestimate the
elasticity of supply; they don't seem to believe, for example,
that higher prices will bring forth more oil, or that increased
supplies will keep oil prices from going through the roof. Nor
do they believe that lifting rent controls in New York will
bring more housing—including existing housing—on the
market.

Price is determined by the interaction of supply and . . .

DEMAND: The quantity of any good that would be bought
at different prices. Generally speaking, the higher the price
of anything, the less of it will be demanded.

One's desire for a good is not the same as one's demand for
it. Desire has to be backed by money and a willingness
to spend the money to become demand. When the price of a

good falls, a person may or may not actually buy more of it, depending on what he thinks an extra unit of that good is worth "at the margin"—on what economists call its "marginal utility."

Characteristically, goods have "diminishing marginal utility"—that is, the more you have of any particular good, the less you are willing to pay for an additional unit of it. If you have one auto, a second car may be worth considerably less to you, and a third may be worth far less than the cost of owning and operating one more car. A few products may seem to possess "increasing marginal utility," so that the more you get, the more you want—like eating pistachio nuts or drinking beer or smoking cigarettes. But sooner or later, diminishing marginal utility appears to set in. Even a billionaire may find that he has no appetite for that seventh villa, that third yacht, or that sixth wife. An exception may be drugs like heroin, on which somebody is "hooked." But these are pathological cases. Avid collectors of art, stamps, or rare books may also be slightly pathological—their appetites grow with consumption, rather than diminish.

Normally consumers, rich, poor, or middle class, vary their consumption patterns in response to prices going up or down for two basic reasons:

THE SUBSTITUTION EFFECT: Using more of a now less expensive product and less of a more expensive one. If gasoline prices and taxes on "gas-guzzling monsters" go up, we may substitute smaller cars for larger ones, extra miles of commuting by bus for commuting in our own cars, or even apartments in town for houses in the suburbs or exurbs. One might even substitute status-enhancing clothes or jewelry for status-enhancing cars.

Shoppers routinely substitute cheaper chicken for dearer veal, Ivory for Duz (or vice versa), etc., juggling new market prices and marginal utilities endlessly.

THE INCOME EFFECT: The effect of a price increase or decrease on the real income of a consumer. A price increase causes one's real income to decline, a price cut makes it rise.

With a price *decrease*, the consumer has more money to spend either on that good or on other goods. Ordinarily, a price cut on a particular good makes it seem like a bargain, and that pleasant experience often leads us to buy more of it. Similarly, a price *increase* is experienced as unpleasant, and usually causes us to buy less of it—unless, as we noted in the case of Giffen's Paradox, the income effect of a price increase is such that one must consume more of the "inferior good" (potatoes or spaghetti or bread) whose prices have risen, as a substitute for the "superior goods" (steak or lobster or entertainment) which one can no longer afford.

The substitution and income effects, taken together, determine the elasticity of demand for any product. The demand for coffee, wine, oil, and food products (taken collectively, not individually) is relatively *inelastic;* producers who realize this often try to restrict supply in order to get or keep their prices up; the Arab oil embargo of 1973 was a perfect demonstration of how, in the face of highly inelastic demand, oil producers were able to restrict supply and greatly raise prices.* Wine growers in France and milk producers in Wisconsin have been known to spill their products on the ground in order to keep prices up, in the face of inelastic de-

---

* The cut in oil supply was only about 10 percent—but oil prices were quadrupled, with slight effect on consumption.

mand. Their aim is to keep a small increase in supply from causing a huge drop in price—and in their own incomes.

THE PRICE MECHANISM: Markets come into equilibrium at the price at which supply (the quantity offered) equals demand (the quantity demanded).

Sellers are satisfied (in the sense that they are selling all they want to sell at that price, and would not want to sell more at a lower price) and all buyers are satisfied (in the sense that they are buying all they want at that price and would not want more at a higher price).

Market prices may move up or down (or remain the same) in response to a host of factors causing shifts in supply (the whole supply curve) or demand (the whole demand curve) or both together.

Bad weather makes prices go up—not just the prices of agricultural products, but of a great many other goods, ranging from steel to nightgowns, because of interruptions of production, breakdowns in transportation, power failures, etc.

Changes in technology cause shifts in supply curves; a more efficient way of making transistors brings down the prices of calculators, computers, radios, television sets, record players, recorders. Increases in the scale of production, as we have seen, often bring down certain product prices.

Shrinking oil and mineral reserves contract supply, and prices move up. "Diseconomies" resulting from shrinking scales of production, as when the market for handmade pocketbooks, horsedrawn carriages, grandfather clocks, custom tailoring, and handmade furniture contracts, push up the prices of such products not only absolutely, but relatively far above what they were in the old days, when skilled labor was cheaper and more abundant.

Similarly, many factors can cause demand curves to swing up or down—booms or busts in the national economy, affecting the incomes of consumers; changes in taste—a President may increase the national taste for chamber music or hominy grits, a popular singer may increase (or decrease) the taste for orange juice; changes in "joint demand"—a fall-off in movie attendance may shrink the demand for popcorn, a rise of interest in skiing may increase the demand for liniment and orthopedic surgery; changes in fashion—the Hamptons may be in, Newport may be out; changes in the seasons, changes in military threats, changes in the livability or stench and danger of cities, changes in the public mood toward hope or despair, excitement or boredom—in brief, changes.

The price mechanism sensitively catches and reacts to all such changes. If equilibrium prices of particular goods move up, more will be produced—because benefits to producers will tend to exceed costs by a wider margin—and human and material resources will tend to shift to those uses.

If equilibrium prices of other goods move down, less of them will be produced, as the cost-benefit ratio for producers is squeezed, and resources shift away to other uses, where the cost-benefit ratios (measured by profits) are higher.

Similarly, consumers will drop out of a market (or buy less in it) as their own cost-benefit ratio declines with a rising price of a particular product. Conversely, they will buy more of a product when their cost-benefit ratio improves.

This is how a market economy allocates its goods and services; the price mechanism constantly flickers out millions and millions of signals. These bits of precisely articulated information help producers to decide what to produce and consumers what to consume, in order to make more money or increase their satisfactions.

INCOME DISTRIBUTION: The price mechanism also is the prime determinant of how income is distributed in a market economy—since income is the return to resources owners (including workers, who own and sell their own labor), as determined in the marketplace. You don't have to like it. But whether you do or not, it is the supply and demand of particular goods and services in the marketplace (backed up by the force of law protecting individual ownership rights) that determine that some rock singer makes a million dollars a year and some professor of microbiology makes thirty thousand dollars and some textile worker seven thousand dollars and some luckless people nothing (unless they get unemployment compensation or welfare).

In the United States, the government takes a hand in changing the distribution of income. It taxes money away from some and transfers it to others. Its purported aim (as through the progressive income tax) is to take relatively more from the rich and (through public education, health, housing, and other programs as well as transfers) give relatively more to the poor. In fact, however, much that government does transfers funds to the middle class or even the rich; for instance, state colleges and universities benefit the middle class or rich much more than they do the poor, and so do Federal housing loans, urban redevelopment programs, highway programs, subsidies for airports and private airplanes, grants for research and the arts, and some programs to preserve wildlife and the woods (where the rich and middle class go, rarely the poor). This does not make such government programs necessarily wrong; the programs may be inherently desirable—and beneficial in the long run also to the poor (if, for example, medical progress is fostered by research grants to the already well-off, or if subsidies to the development of solar energy ultimately protect the jobs and increase the living standards of the poor as well). Virtually every organized group in the society, from oil drillers to doctors to lawyers to farmers to workers to bankers to college professors to defense producers to old people to welfare recipients seeks to use the Federal government to increase its share of national income for allegedly worthy reasons.

But it is the operation of the market that fundamentally determines the distribution of income, although the role of government has grown increasingly important in shaping patterns. While government in the United States has not imposed an upper ceiling on individual incomes, it has put a rough floor under the lowest incomes. No one need starve or lack clothing, shelter, or health care—if he or she knows how to get help, which is a considerable *if*.

It is not only through government that various private groups attempt to alter the distribution of income in their favor. Discrimination against minority workers or women increases the take of male white workers, and some unions, whether openly or covertly, favor such discrimination. Management groups or university faculties may do (and in the past have done) the same. Government, through the equal-opportunity laws, tries to correct such discrimination.

The chief way that private groups seek to increase their

share of income is by augmenting their monopoly power in the market.

MONOPOLY: A market structure in which there is complete control by one seller of the production or sale of a product or service. Those who praise monopoly say it permits strong firms to do research, be nice to their workers and benefit society. Those who damn it say it milks consumers and leads to excessively concentrated political as well as economic power.

COMPETITION: The opposite of monopoly—a market in which many suppliers contend for sales and many consumers contend for available goods. Competition is considered a good way of keeping suppliers on their toes and passing benefits along to consumers. The foes of competition always insist that they are trying to prevent "cutthroat" competition —stores that underprice "unfairly," osteopathic physicians who take clients away from M.D.s, foreign producers who "dump" their goods at prices below costs, gypsy taxi drivers who are breaking the fee structure of licensed cabs and allegedly taking bread out of the mouths of the children of legitimate cab drivers, etc. The simple rule is: Monopolists hate competition.

MONOPOLISTIC COMPETITION: The halfway house between monopoly and competition; monopolistic competition is where things are in most major American industries.

The question is how concentrated an industry must be before its market power is to be deemed injurious to the public interest. Alternatively, when can an industry be regarded as "workably" competitive? The antitrust authorities and the courts are supposed to sort out that difficult issue. They tackle it hesitantly, torn between the goals of efficiency and equity, a fundamental conflict within a mixed economy.

EFFICIENCY VERSUS EQUITY—AND OTHER SOCIAL GOALS: Lovers of the market system say its glory is its efficiency; it gives the most output for any given set of resources. But critics contend that markets are not necessarily "fair" (they may reward the greedy or tricky, not the good or even the socially valuable). And, add the critics, market prices do not take account of the undesirable social effects of production— such "externalities" as filth, contamination of water and air, urban congestion, ruin of land (as from strip mining), or the depletion of natural resources. Nor, they say, does the market price provide a reward for *favorable* externalities, such as housing that improves the whole community, or the growth of skills and knowledge that results from a company's research and training programs, so that such effects are underproduced relative to social need.

Markets are criticized for distributing income unequally and arbitrarily; excessively large rewards go, say the critics, to those who got to a country first—and their heirs. The critics contend that in advanced capitalist economies markets are dominated by producers and stacked against consumer interests.

The defenders of capitalism sometimes concede that markets are imperfect, but they say that other systems are marked by complete domination of consumers by producers. In Communist countries, the state is the sole monopolist and the sole check on its own powers, as the following dispatch from Malcolm Browne to *The New York Times* (dated July 19, 1977) indicates:

MOSCOW—The Soviet leadership today ordered the bureaucracy to provide more attractive food, goods, and services, while reducing the number of surly waitresses and shopkeepers with which citizens must contend.

A joint party and government directive voiced the Kremlin's displeasure with the indifferent goods and services available in the Soviet Union and elaborated goals for improving matters. But it did not specify exactly how the proposed new era of consumer welfare was to be brought about and how it was to be financed.

The directive, covering six columns of print in the party newspaper *Pravda*, simply ordered government agencies to provide more seats in restaurants, more storage facilities for food, better designed and more attractive packaging, semiprepared convenience foods and especially frozen foods, shopping centers, vending machines and home delivery service of complete meals.

The basic decisions concerning the allocation of government investment to consumer goods and the actual supply of goods are determined for five years at a time by the State Planning Committee. . . .

Among the specific criticisms voiced in the latest directive were these:

The quality of service in stores and public eating places is falling short of the increased needs of the population.

The distribution for sale of some products is permitted to deteriorate, even while these products are available in warehouses.

There are cases of rude and intolerable treatment of customers.

Many manufacturers continue to produce outdated designs for which there is no demand.

Consumerism obviously has its work cut out for it in the Communist world.

But can bureaucrats change the situation much simply by commanding underlings to provide better service and to show more sensitivity to consumers' needs? It seems improbable, because all power rests in the hands of producers, both top dogs and underlings. A command system has difficulty in distributing rewards and providing economic incentives for the host of small daily actions that add up to good service and attention to consumer needs and tastes. Can Orders of Lenin or good-conduct medals do the job for the hosts of salespeople and producers involved? Awarding the medals is, after all, a command function that doesn't change the system. Can *fear* be as efficient as the desire for personal gain and the daily pressures of the marketplace? Not likely.

PRIVATE GOODS AND PUBLIC GOODS: Critics of capitalism assert, however, that it is loaded in favor of such "private" goods as autos, soap, deodorants, watches, refrigerators, clothing, etc., and against "public goods," such as public television, public beaches, concert halls, museums, symphony orchestras, ballets, parks, hospitals, medical services, public schools, or decent homes for the aged. Private goods are favored by the market system, say its critics, because they are easier to produce, package, sell—and make a profit on.

But champions of the market system say private goods are what customers really want. Given a free choice, they assert, people always prefer to spend their own money on whatever they prefer, rather than pay higher taxes and have the government spend it for them, allegedly in their own best interests.

The critics respond that people have been "brainwashed" by advertising, and corrupted by the all-pervasive commercial culture and by their desires for status and the attributes of material success. Public goods are slighted by market systems, say the critics, because they are hard to sell to individual customers. Since everyone shares public goods, each individual thinks, "If I don't pay for my small share (of a park, a school system, or public TV) it won't matter much. I won't get less of it. Let somebody else pay."

But the champions of capitalism maintain that Communist societies don't do any better on public goods than do capitalist societies; if anything, they say, the Communists are less sensitive to pollution and environmental considerations, less efficient in providing public services to citizens, because they are more secretive, less democratic, less subject to being cast out by the electorate. Indeed, public goods in totalitarian societies are evaluated as to whether they will enhance the power and prolong the regime of the political authorities and the bureaucracy, not whether they serve the interests of ordinary people.

However, the priorities accorded to public versus private goods are not simply a matter of consumer choices and voter decisions in capitalist countries. It was President Eisenhower, once General Eisenhower, who warned against the emergence of a "military-industrial complex." "This conjunction of an immense military establishment and a large arms industry," he said, "is new in the American experience. The total influence—economic, political, even spiritual—is felt in every city, every state-house, every office of the Federal Government. We recognize the imperative need for this development. Yet we must not fail to comprehend its grave implications. Our toil, resources, and livelihood are all involved; so is the very structure of our society."

Yet the taxpayers in the United States exert considerable pressure upon government not to spend too much on the military. It may be that a market system that conditions people to regard private goods as highly desirable personal benefits, and public goods, whether military or social, as unwelcome burdens, to be paid for by an inequitable tax system, underspends on genuine public needs.

But the champions of the market insist that public goods are overpraised by intellectuals, and are overfunded and overproduced in any system where politicians and bureaucrats have too much power—whether the system is called capitalist or Communist. With all its imperfections, they maintain, the market is still a better guide than the state to what the public really wants, and a better guarantor of efficiency in its production and fairness in its distribution.

Ultimately, the issue may be one of ideology versus philosophy:

IDEOLOGY: False ideas held by your opponents; a rationalization of their interest positions.

PHILOSOPHY: What you believe.

CHAPTER SIX

The National Economy

What causes a nation's economy to expand or contract? What causes inflation and unemployment? How does a national economy grow over the long run? And how can a nation's economic health and performance be improved? Those are the main questions involved in macroeconomics, the branch of economics that studies the national economy as a whole.

THE FALLACY OF COMPOSITION: It is often mistakenly assumed that what is true for the parts of a system is true for the system as a whole. If you stand up at a football game, you can see better, but if everybody stands up nobody can see better.

In economics, if you, as an individual, decide to save more

out of your income, you will increase your wealth. But if everyone in the nation tries to save more out of income, this may reduce national wealth—by reducing, in succession, sales, the production of goods, the incomes of producers and their employees, and ultimately national saving and investment.

If you, as an individual, are able to raise your prices, that may be a good thing for your business. But if every business does the same, the obvious result will be inflation, a bad thing for the nation.

Balancing the budget so that outgo does not exceed income may be a sound rule for you and your family. But budget balancing does not always make sense for the national government; for the government to do so during a business slump when unemployment is rising would worsen the slump and increase unemployment.

Cutting wage rates may enable one employer to hire more workers; but cutting the wages of all workers may lead to fewer, not more, jobs—since workers would have less to spend on goods.

Thus, when we shift from micro- to macroeconomics, some key concepts change. The fundamental concepts of macroeconomics are not *supply* and *demand*, as in microeconomics, but *aggregate supply* and *aggregate demand*.

AGGREGATE SUPPLY: The capacity of a nation's total resources, at full employment, to produce goods and services. Aggregate supply is more or less fixed at any given time, but it can grow over time—as the labor force grows, industry invests in new plant and equipment, the government builds more schools, highways, airports, and other capital goods—and as science, technology, and human knowledge advance.

In the short run, however, aggregate supply sets a limit on what the economy can produce, a limit that may or may not be exceeded by . . .

AGGREGATE DEMAND: All the money that people, businesses, and governments spend on goods and services. Instability and hardship in a national economy result when aggregate demand and aggregate supply get out of whack.

INFLATION: The form instability takes when aggregate demand grows more rapidly than aggregate supply, yanking up the general level of prices; this is "demand-pull inflation." An excessive increase in the supply of money causes total demand to increase too much, and hence causes inflation.

Inflation may also result from the pressures of labor, industrial monopolies, or international cartels, driving up costs faster than productivity; this is "cost-push inflation." Expectations of inflation may be a self-fulfilling prophecy as every seller of goods and services raises prices and wages in an effort to keep ahead of the game; as the wheel spins on and on, this is known as "momentum inflation."

UNEMPLOYMENT: The form that instability takes when aggregate demand falls below aggregate supply; this creates a "capacity gap," with part of the nation's labor force and some of its industrial plant standing idle.

The demand for labor is a "derived demand"—that is, derived from the demand for goods and services. The way to cure mass unemployment is to expand the total demand for the goods and services that the economy is capable of producing.

Unemployment also results, in the case of particular workers, from other factors, such as lack of education or skills that employers can use and are willing to pay for, or job discrimination against blacks, older people, or women, or minimum wage laws that set wages above the productive value of some workers, such as inexperienced teen-agers.

Urban decay, social unrest, and crime doubtless contribute to unemployment. Employers may move their plants or offices away from troubled city centers to the suburbs or other states, and workers may be unable to follow because of family circumstances or inadequate transportation or housing in the new area.

Rundown regions, such as Appalachia or parts of New England, may suffer high unemployment due to industrial stagnation and the immobility of labor.

Unemployment resulting from social, locational, technological, and specific market factors unrelated to overall weakness in the economy is called *structural* unemployment.

But when unemployment increases by the hundreds of thousands or millions over the course of a single year, you can be sure the change is due not to structural factors but to a business slump—and insufficient aggregate demand.

The waste due to inefficient use of resources may be greatly exceeded by the waste due to involuntary unemployment. A person working inefficiently is obviously producing more than a person standing idle.

FISCAL AND MONETARY POLICY: The two basic ways of trying to bring aggregate demand into balance with aggregate supply, and thereby to prevent either inflation or unemployment.

MONETARY POLICY: The regulation by the Federal Reserve System (or Fed, as it is called for short) of the nation's money supply and interest rates.

In the United States, about one-fourth of all the money used to make payments consists of currency—coins and bills —and three-fourths consists of checks drawn against "demand deposits" in commercial banks.

United States currency is minted by the Treasury and distributed to private commercial banks by the Fed. The amount of currency put into circulation depends on how much cash individuals and businesses want to hold in the form of coins or bills.

Commercial banks can, in effect, create money by making loans to their customers (loans create demand deposits against which the borrowers can draw). But, by manipulating the reserves of the banking system, the Fed regulates *how much money* the banks can create—or must extinguish.

MONEY SUPPLY: The *narrow* definition of the money supply (M-1) includes demand deposits at all commercial banks (other than government and interbank deposits, and foreign demand balances at Federal Reserve Banks) plus currency in circulation (that is, currency held by individuals and businesses, but not currency stored in the Department of the Treasury, Federal Reserve Banks, and the vaults of commercial banks).

The *broad* definition of the money supply (M-2) adds time and savings deposits to the demand deposits and currency in circulation included in M-1. (The New York and St. Louis Federal Reserve Banks issue data on weekly changes in M-1 and M-2.)

M-1 is the money that is used to buy goods and services. But time and savings deposits can readily be converted into the demand deposits and currency of M-1, and demand deposits and currency, by the same token, can readily be converted into the time and savings deposits of M-2. Hence, one should pay attention to both M-1 and M-2 to see how the money supply is growing.

OPEN-MARKET OPERATIONS: The Fed regulates the money supply chiefly by buying or selling government securities in the "open market"—that is, through security dealers, banks, businesses, and individual persons.

When the Fed is worried about *inflation,* it tightens up the money supply by *selling* government securities. This reduces the reserves of the banks and cuts their ability to make loans to the public.

When the Fed is worried about *unemployment* and a sagging economy, it *buys* government securities in the open market and thereby expands the money supply. This increases the reserves of the banks and their ability to make loans. And if individuals and businesses borrow more, this swells the aggregate demand for goods and services, and hence for labor.

CHANGING RESERVE REQUIREMENTS: The Fed can also spur or retard the economy by changing the ratio of reserves that a commercial bank is required to hold against deposits. An increase in reserve requirements reduces the bank's lending ability, curbs the growth of the money supply, and checks inflation. A decrease in reserve requirements does the reverse: it increases the bank's ability to lend, spurs growth of the money supply, and tends to increase employment.

INTEREST-RATE POLICY: The Fed can also try to manage the economy by influencing changes in interest rates. Lower interest rates encourage borrowing, higher rates deter it. Interest rates—the price of money—are particularly important in affecting the demand for housing, autos, and other goods bought on credit.

The Fed can exert some influence on interest rates, both indirectly and directly. Indirectly, it can push interest rates up by making money "tight"—that is, by decreasing the growth of the money supply, causing borrowers to bid up the price of money. Directly, the Fed controls two key rates of interest—the Federal funds rate (which commercial banks charge each other for overnight loans) and the discount rate (which the Fed charges member banks that wish to borrow from it to replenish their reserves).

The Fed may use the Fed-funds rate or the discount rate to let the banks know that it wants other interest rates to move up or down. The Fed usually asserts that it really follows the market; but the market often follows the Fed.

Federal Reserve officials contend that, at least in the longer run, it is the expectations of borrowers and lenders about the business outlook, and particularly about inflation, that determine whether interest rates rise or fall. Fears of inflation tend to push interest rates up, as lenders seek extra compensation for the loss of the value of their money, and borrowers, expecting to gain as prices rise, are willing to pay more. Conversely, a slowing of inflation tends to bring interest rates down. So the Fed insists that the only way it can act to prevent high and rising interest rates—so unpopular with Congressmen, stockbrokers, investors, home buyers, and others—is by preventing inflation; that is, by keeping the money supply from growing too fast. The Fed's critics often attack it for increasing the money supply too slowly, with excess unemployment and sluggish economic growth or recession the result.

FISCAL POLICY: Actions taken by the Federal government to stabilize the economy by increasing or decreasing Federal spending, increasing or decreasing taxes, and increasing or decreasing the deficit or surplus in the Federal budget.

The President makes the basic plan for fiscal policy when he submits his budget to Congress every year in late January. Congress, which has the power of the purse under the Constitution, either gives the President about what he wants or struggles to alter his budget, depending on its judgment on national needs and priorities—with the Congressional Budget Office to advise it on what would make a sensible fiscal policy to spur the economy or moderate it. The Federal Reserve has no official role in fiscal policy—though Fed chairmen have often engaged in a good deal of criticism of the Administration's or Congress's fiscal actions.

Constructing the national budget involves much more than deciding whether the economy needs to be stimulated or retarded. The budget is the principal national mechanism for allocating resources to the public sector or the private, and for determining priorities within the public sector. But the particular budgetary decisions on spending and taxes also need to be interrelated in order to measure their total impact on the national economy. The budget plays a major role in stabilizing or destabilizing the nation's economy.

The basic fiscal policy rules for stabilization can be simply stated:

· *If the economy is suffering from inflation caused by*

excess aggregate demand, reduce government spending or increase tax rates, or both.

• *If the economy is suffering from unemployment caused by too little aggregate demand, increase government spending, reduce tax rates, or both.*

STAGFLATION: Economic stagnation combined with inflation.

What should fiscal policy be when the economy is suffering from the economic disease of simultaneous inflation and unemployment? The treatment will require some combination of economic balance, juggling, guessing, luck, improvisation, and specific measures aimed at specific aspects of inflation and unemployment.

In dealing with stagflation, you must first decide whether inflation or unemployment is the more serious problem and whether the economy is moving toward worse inflation or worse unemployment.

If inflation is seen as the greater menace, national fiscal and monetary policy should be aimed at restraint. But if unemployment is held to be the greater danger, fiscal and monetary stimulus should be applied. Republicans usually favor restraint, Democrats stimulus.

Setting aggregate demand so that it is neither too strong nor too weak—a fine line that may be impossible to find—does not give the whole answer to how to deal with stagflation. If inflation persists, even without excess aggregate demand, specific attacks should be launched on the forces pushing up wages and prices faster than productivity.

Efforts could be made to increase productivity as a means of curbing inflation; for instance, you might call for an investment tax credit or more liberal depreciation allowances to induce industry to invest more in productive equipment. But raising national productivity is extremely tough to do, especially in the short run.

How to stop an ongoing inflationary spiral without putting the economy into recession is an unsolved problem. Direct wage and price controls may have some shock value, but are likely to become less effective and more disturbing to the economy as time goes by. And nowadays they lack political support. Direct controls go against the free-enterprise philosophy of the Republicans—and against the political interests of the Democrats. Labor, strong in the Democratic camp, opposes wage controls, fearing that it will lose ground, because wages are easier to control than prices—with the employers to help do the controlling. And business interests, which have considerable clout in the Democratic as well as Republican party, are against price controls because they see them as a blow to profits, a source of inefficiency, and a curb to their own autonomy.

Yet both Democratic and Republican Administrations, under the lash of inflation and the pressures of adversely affected voters, keep looking for methods to curb the market power of business and labor. Presidents resort to "jawboning"—public or private lecturing—and other types of "open mouth" policy. They seek to set standards ("guidelines" or "guideposts") for noninflationary wage and price decisions. The hope is that labor and management can somehow be led to accept noninflationary wage and price standards on a voluntary basis. Thus far it has seemed like a vain hope.

Stagflation also calls forth a host of proposals for reducing unemployment by means other than a more rapid increase in aggregate demand (which, it is feared, would worsen the inflation). Among the proposed means of attacking structural unemployment are: public-service job programs; youth-employment programs; attacks on racial discrimination and other restrictive practices, such as archaic building codes and apprenticeship rules; Federal subsidies to cities without the financial means of maintaining adequate police, fire, educational, and other services; welfare reform, to encourage those on welfare to seek employment without a dollar-for-dollar loss of welfare benefits; community services, such as day care for young children, that would enable more parents on welfare to work.

Some economists are skeptical about the ability of such programs to solve the structural unemployment problem, and they believe that more emphasis should be put on eliminating the minimum wage, which keeps young and low-productivity workers out of jobs.

Others think the best way to get rid of structural unemployment is not by creating public jobs for the unemployed (as Arthur Okun puts it, "injecting the needle right in your sore throat") but by increasing the aggregate demand for goods, services, and labor, while using "incomes policy" to prevent inflation. Incomes policy refers to measures aimed at keeping the growth of incomes in line with the real growth of output. Thus, wage "guidelines" may specify that workers should increase their wages by only as much as national productivity grows—by about 3 percent per year. Other guidelines or controls may be laid down for prices, interest payments, rents, profits, dividends, which are all forms of income.

Thus far it can confidently, although regretfully, be said, the stagflation problem has not been cracked, either in the United States or in Western Europe. Both inflation and unemployment dog the European economies after their long postwar boom; countries like Germany and Switzerland, which once were heavy importers of foreign labor from southern Europe, now send those workers back home (somewhat alleviating their own unemployment but increasing unemployment in southern Europe).

The mysterious ailment called stagflation saps a nation's . . .

ECONOMIC GROWTH: The expansion over a period of years of an economy's capacity to produce real goods and services.

The concept of economic growth is based on an analogy with biological growth, which has been defined as a process, indirectly resulting from chemical, osmotic, and other forces, by which material is introduced into the organism and transferred from one part of it to another, so that the organism expands. Economic growth involves similar processes in economic organisms. But what is an economic organism? It's not the flow of goods and services that issues forth every year (or every day or hour), but the complex of people, factories, stores, farms, rivers, dams, banks and underlying ideas that produces the stream of goods and services.

What are the forces that determine the growth of the economic organism? To what extent can they be altered?

Economic growth is the result of two basic sets of causes. One is a set of cultural forces, including science, technology, population changes, religion, politics, and social attitudes toward work, material possessions, etc. The other is a set of economic factors affecting the possibility of accumulating capital funds and investing them in goods-producing equipment.

These two sets of forces, cultural and economic, must be joined if growth is to occur. The two come together in the act of investment; that is the genetic moment for economic growth. To provide the resources for investment, individuals, businesses, and the economy as a whole must refrain from consuming all of current output; that is the act of *saving*. But it is *investment* that translates saved resources into productive equipment and technology, and causes the economy to grow.

Economists divide investment into two broad categories: autonomous and induced. Autonomous investment creates its own demand; induced investment represents a response to already existing demand that forces producers to increase capacity. Autonomous investment results chiefly from new techniques of production, which cut production costs; new products, which open up new markets; new resources, which themselves often result from new technology; population growth and migration; and wars—or the "moral equivalent" of wars, such as energy crises, rioting in cities, starvation in poor countries, or "cold wars"—contests between economic systems for hegemony over third countries.

Induced investment, developing from factors within an economic system, results primarily from changes in the level of business activity, and from the relationship of costs, prices, interest rates, and profits. An economy operating far below existing capacity stifles investment; during the Great Depression, net investment fell to zero and below—that is, we lived off past investment, ran down existing plant and equipment.

Although economic growth represents the *capacity* of the economy to produce (the *stock* of its productive resources), it is customarily measured by changes in . . .

GROSS NATIONAL PRODUCT (GNP): the *flow* of current production—the value of goods and services produced by the economy as a whole over a given time period, such as one year.

GNP is measured in two different ways: (1) the money spent to buy the output or (2) the money received for producing the output. The first is called the *flow-of-product* method; the second the *earnings-and-cost* method. Theoretically the two should always be equal—a dollar spent by a consumer equals a dollar received by a producer and spent for labor, electricity, advertising, or retained as profit.

In computing GNP, economists count only the production of final goods and services—the final product that reaches the consumer. For instance, GNP would include only the value of the packaged loaves of bread consumers have bagged at the checkout counter in a supermarket—not the gross receipts of the farmers who grew the wheat, the millers, the shippers, the packagers, the advertisers, the wholesalers, and everyone else involved in producing the final loaves of bread. The final value of the bread equals not the gross sales but the "value added" by everyone involved in the production process.

GNP can be measured either in "current dollars"—dollars measured at what they can currently purchase—or in "constant dollars"—dollars corrected for inflation relative to some base period. GNP in current dollars is also called "nominal GNP," and GNP in constant dollars is also called "real GNP." (The reader in quest of data on nominal and real

GNP is referred to the Appendix on page 184.) Real GNP is computed by dividing nominal GNP by a price index called "the GNP deflator"; this measures a sample of prices covering the whole national economy.

There are four major components of GNP: (1) consumer spending on final goods and services; (2) business outlays on investment and consumer outlays on new housing; (3) government spending on goods and services; and (4) net exports —the difference between exports and imports.

GNP is a useful measure of total economic activity, but not of changes in social well-being. For instance, GNP counts the output of chemicals that pollute air and water the same as equipment to clean up air and water. GNP counts handguns that kill the same as medicine to save life. It does not discriminate between the values of cigarettes and vitamins. GNP puts no value at all on leisure time. And GNP data are not corrected for the destruction of natural resources.

The analysis of past changes in GNP and its components provides a basis for forecasting the national economy.

ECONOMIC FORECASTING: Divining the future. How do economists forecast?[1] The basic techniques of the art of prophecy have not changed much since ancient times; everything one can say about the future must be based on knowledge about the present and the past.

Economists still use what may be called "the loaded deck" technique—the assumption that the future has already been determined. The stock market is in an uptrend right now, so the trend will continue. The consumer is spending more, so the consumer can be expected to go on spending more. Business is hopeful, so business will continue hopeful—and capital spending will recover. (This is all not quite as loony as it sounds; trends *do* continue—until they change. The safest prediction about tomorrow's weather is that it will not be too different from today's.)

Then there is the symptomatic or "straws in the wind" technique of prediction—the reading of thermometers, barometers, and economic indicators (statistical series that plot the business cycle). The index of leading indicators is up, says the economist, so there is a good chance that business will move up. But you can be sure of this only when the movement of the leading indicators has been confirmed by the coincident and lagging indicators.* (Seems like a safe enough tautology.)

Next there is the form book. Many economists follow the humorist James Thurber and say, "You could look it up." For example, "America's economic recoveries have, since Tojo's war, run for an average of 34 months. By this ready reckoning the current recovery, now 28 months old, is nearing senility" (*The Economist*, August 6, 1977).

* Among the leading indicators (those that move in advance of the business cycle) are: the average work week in manufacturing, job placements in industry, net business formations, new orders for durable goods, contracts and orders for plant and equipment, new building permits, industrial materials prices, stock prices, corporate profits after taxes, ratio of prices to unit labor costs in manufacturing, and changes in consumer installment debt.

The coincident indicators (those that roughly coincide with the business cycle) include: employees in nonagricultural establishments, the unemployment rate, gross national product in constant dollars, industrial production, personal income, manufacturing and trade sales, and sales of retail stores.

The lagging indicators (those that lag behind the business cycle) include: the unemployment rate of persons out of work for fifteen weeks or more, business expenditures on plant and equipment, the book value of manufacturing and trade inventories, labor cost per unit of output in manufacturing, commercial and industrial loans outstanding, and bank rates on short-term business loans.

All these indicators are logged in a United States Government publication called *Business Cycle Developments*.

More profoundly, say the scholars of the form book, history is cyclical; it waxeth as it waneth. Economic philos ophers can always cite history to suit their purposes, as the Devil cites scripture and the statisticians cite statistics.

Modern mathematical economists ("econometricians") nowadays employ, for forecasting purposes, the most impressive black magic of all: science, out of the bowels of the computer. Econometricians say: "Regard this dynamic model, derived from masses of empirical data, tracing the interrelationships of many variables. It will yield quantitative outputs when you feed it quantitative inputs."

An econometric model for forecasting the national economy is really a set of equations. The knowns (present facts or assumptions) in the equations are used as a means of deriving the unknowns (the future level of GNP, employment, unemployment, the price level, housing construction, profits, etc.). For instance, one equation might tell you that consumption will depend on income (our old "consumption function") plus some other factors.

Another equation might tell you that business investment will depend on last year's profits, current interest rates, and other variables.

A third equation might describe the future course of government spending, derived particularly from presently available information on the government budget. And so on.

Taken together, and solved together, all these equations will give you a picture of the future based on presently available information and past relationships among economic variables.

The econometric models, however huge and sophisticated, rarely disclose anything surprising or dramatic about the future. By shifting the assumptions on which they are based, the forecasts can be made more optimistic or more pessimistic. But businessmen and government officials, who must make decisions that reach into the future, regard them as better than nothing. The "standard forecast" at least offers a reasonable basis for planning, if everything goes according to Hoyle.

Some economists distrust and even despise the huge econometric models and believe that simple, positive economic laws are better and will prevail. "OPEC will break up and oil prices will come down," predicts a Chicago free-market economist. "A price set above the market by a cartel must lead to oversupply and underconsumption. Then OPEC will split. No cartel has ever lasted." The only thing the free-market positivists cannot predict is when their prediction will come true. They regard this as a minor defect.

Finally there are the seers who base their forecasts not on economic laws but on insights—political insights, psychological insights, experienced, personal, insightful insights. "Jimmy Carter will be more conservative than anyone assumes. He is really a small spender," says one insightful seer.

"Mr. Carter will revert to type," says another. "He is really a populist. Wait till he gets some popular reaction to the persistence of high unemployment, especially with an election around the corner, and watch what he does. And wait till prices start moving up faster—you won't be able to distinguish his incomes policy from direct controls."

"Does anybody really know what President Carter will do?" ask the skeptics. "Does Jimmy Carter know?"

More fundamentally, one may ask, does it matter all that much? Does the American economy wait there, like an inanimate machine, for the President to throw the switch and turn up the dials?

Clearly, the movements of the American economy depend on much more than Presidential speeches or even fiscal and monetary policies, as past Presidents have discovered. There is some sort of "natural" or organic process of economic change that emerges from the variables of the real world in a way analogous to the simultaneous equations of an econometric model; and it can run on and oscillate, unaffected by the touch of Washington's hands.

The private economy's business cycle existed long before there was a "political cycle." But now there *is* a political cycle superimposed on the private business cycle, pushing it down, thrusting it up, as politicians and government officials try to manage the national economy.

CHAPTER SEVEN
The World Economy

Diagnosing the world economy and its problems involves the use of both microeconomics and macroeconomics. Microeconomics is needed to analyze world markets for oil, sugar, steel, textiles, autos, computers, and other internationally traded goods, as well as flows of foreign investment. Macroeconomics, applied to large areas rather than just a single nation, is needed to explain inflation, unemployment, economic growth or decay throughout the world.

Special problems arise in the world economy because sovereignty is divided among many nations. The sovereign states can and often do interfere in many ways with the movement of goods, money, and people across national borders.

INTERNATIONAL MONEY (OR FOREIGN EXCHANGE): Anything that is acceptable to discharge debts between the people or businesses or governments of one country and those of another. The many different nations create not only a Babel of languages but of moneys. In fact, money is really a form of language—a remarkably precise and, at the same time, remarkably *imprecise* form of language. A piece of paper money has a simple cardinal number printed on it, but that number does not indicate the value of the bill. The true worth of each bill is ratio: this dollar or this mark or this peso or this krona in relation to the prices of all goods and services that these different currencies can buy at home or abroad. And all those prices are constantly changing, not only in their "average" level, however calculated, but in relation to each other, and hence to the dollars, marks, pesos, kronor, etc., held by a particular person.

Money is not just language; it is also a contract. A United States dollar or German mark is exchanged between a person or a firm that offers something for sale—say, a box of strawberries or an electrical generator—and a person or firm that buys it. But the purchaser by implication promises the seller that he can get something of equal value later with the money he accepts. Only it will not be the purchaser of the goods who will make good that promise. It will be somebody else, somebody who had nothing to do with the original contract. The promise will not be kept precisely.

Who stands behind the contract? The nation-state. But the state is a notoriously untrustworthy character. And all the states, with all their different moneys acting in discordant concert, are even more untrustworthy—not because they are led by evil men and women but because the problems of exchange is so damned difficult and complicated. The dollar that buys a stein of beer in Munich must become a mark, or rather two-and-a-fraction marks. And very likely, before pesos from Mexico City can buy beer in Munich, they first become dollars, then become marks, and eventually, if the game is to go on, become dollars again and then pesos again (which is necessary to keep the Mexican and German and United States balances of payments in some sort of order).

The Once Almighty Dollar

It is the dollar that remains the kingpin of the world monetary system, though it is more wobbly on its throne than it was just after World War II. The United States emerged from the war as the strongest economy in the world and the natural leader of the non-Communist nations; its fundamental mission was to lead its wartime allies and its former enemies, Germany and Japan, toward reconstruction and economic growth. This mission was considered by American internationalists crucial to the future expansion of the United States and world economies and to the resuscitation of the enfeebled nations of Europe and Asia.

That brilliant job of resuscitation is now taken for granted, but no one who in those days saw the grim, shattered cities of Europe and Asia, the disease and famine, the desperate mood, and the corruption of the people can ever forget it. In the decades after the war, the world economy experienced the greatest upsurge of growth in all history. World trade revived, and the world monetary system was rebuilt as the United States deliberately incurred deficits in its balance of payments in order to feed dollars and gold to the world. In effect, the United States was acting like the big winner in a poker game who knows that unless the poker chips are redistributed, the game is over.

Those deliberately incurred American deficits made the best of sense, both for the United States and for the rest of the world. The concept of an interdependent world economy was no mere intellectual abstraction, but the basis for shared prosperity and growth.

So the reconstructed world economy and monetary system was founded on the strength of the American economy, on the strength of the dollar, and on the deficits in the United States balance of payments—that is, the gap between the outflow and inflow of dollars.

Therein lay a serious contradiction: A strong dollar and chronic deficits in the United States balance of payments would in time prove to be incompatible; either the dollar would weaken or the American deficits would have to be ended. There was a further contradiction: If the American deficits ended, the flow of dollars that was providing the monetary reserves for world economic expansion would also cease.

In fact, when the United States decided in the late 1950's that the reconstruction period was over, it turned out to be extremely hard to end the deficits. One reason was that the United States was reluctant to give up its role as leader of the non-Communist world. The twentieth century had acquired the billing, at least in the United States, as "the American century." Both the Korean and Vietnam wars signified American determination to carry the "free world's burdens" —the equivalent of Britain's "white man's burden" a century earlier.

America's persistent payments deficits were not due solely to its military actions and economic aid programs. Of growing importance, as the deficits went on year after year, was the overvaluation of the United States dollar in relation to gold and to other currencies. This hurt American exports and made imports, as well as foreign travel and foreign investment, cheaper for Americans. So the migration of American business overseas went on apace, with corporations using abundant and overvalued dollars to buy up foreign assets, start branches and subsidiaries abroad, hire foreign labor, and use other foreign resources to increase their worldwide profits.

Foreigners, in the midst of the dollar prosperity, were schizoid about the trend. Many, especially those in close partnership with the Americans, welcomed the growth that United States capital, technology, and managerial know-how helped bring. But there was increasing concern in Europe about the inflation that the rapid dollar inflow was also helping to breed. And there was growing opposition to the "American challenge" of economic and political dominance —and about the recklessness of American military policy.

The End of Bretton Woods

Vietnam particularly strained the political bonds between the United States and its European allies. It also sealed the doom of the postwar world monetary system that had been built on a strong dollar and fixed exchange rates between the dollar, gold, and all other currencies.

The Bretton Woods Agreement of 1944, which established the postwar monetary system, had required every country joining the International Monetary Fund to pick a par value for its currency in terms of gold (whether it actually had any gold or not). The United States, which had most of the world's gold reserves, said it would keep the par value of the dollar at 1/35 of an ounce of gold (where President Roosevelt had set it in 1933—before then it had been worth 1/21 of an ounce). So gold was officially priced at $35 to an ounce of gold, and all other countries picked par values for their moneys in relation to the dollar and gold.

But the persistent outflow of dollars was undermining the value of the dollar in relation to gold and other currencies. The Vietnam war accelerated the outflow of dollars from the United States and, even more damaging to the dollar, President Lyndon B. Johnson unleashed inflation at home by his unwillingness to ask Congress either for a tax increase to pay for the Vietnam war or to cut his Great Society spending programs to make room for the war in the Federal budget.

President Nixon inherited the inflation—and eventually made it worse. After a year of trying to stop inflation by tight money alone, Mr. Nixon brought the country a recession. Finding rising unemployment combined with a hangover of inflation politically intolerable—especially with the 1972 Congressional elections looming—he switched to a highly expansive fiscal and monetary policy (the Federal Reserve was sympathetic to his goals). For political reasons, he announced—few politicians had ever made it so explicit—"I am now a Keynesian." That is, he intended to expand aggregate demand to achieve full employment. But to prevent that expansive fiscal and monetary policy from causing inflation, President Nixon, on August 15, 1971, clamped on wage and price controls.

Under Nixonian management, the United States balance-of-payments deficit had worsened. Dollars had poured out of the country; so, as part of his August 15 "New Economic Policy," Mr. Nixon also slammed shut the gold window of the United States, refusing to pay out any more gold to foreign claimants in exchange for their surplus dollars. Nevertheless, overvalued dollars continued to gush out as expectations of what once would have been unthinkable—a dollar devaluation—grew. Finally, on December 18, 1971, at an extraordinary monetary conference at the Smithsonian Institution in Washington, held under the aegis of the ten richest nations amid the trappings and relics of the greatest achievements of American technology, the dollar was devalued by 8 percent.

The object of the Smithsonian conference, from the American standpoint, was to devalue the dollar enough to produce equilibrium or, if possible, a big surplus in the American balance of payments. This would, it was hoped, restore American economic power and prestige; it would also save the "dollar standard," with the United States as monarch of the world monetary system. For this reason the Nixon Administration was eager not to "devalue the dollar" officially, but to make other governments upvalue their currencies.

Logically, there would seem to be no difference between devaluing one currency and upvaluing others in relation to it—and indeed there is virtually none. However, there was one important difference. The dollar had been regarded as the fixed star of the world monetary system, the star around which all the other national currencies revolved. For the dollar to change its own value—to be devalued in relation to other moneys and to gold—would symbolize a radical change in the conception of the world monetary order, like the Copernican revolution in which the earth was no longer seen as the unchanging center of the universe.

The Movable Dollar

After the Smithsonian devaluation of the dollar, no matter how much the Americans might insist that the dollar was still the fixed center of the world monetary system, the skeptics would go on saying, like Galileo, "But it does move." And in fact, after the Smithsonian agreement, United States officials themselves gradually accepted the new concept of a movable dollar.

The Smithsonian agreement—the "greatest monetary agreement in the history of the world," Richard Nixon called it—was supposed to be a one-shot realignment of exchange rates that would preserve the fixed-exchange-rate system created at Bretton Woods. But the Smithsonian agreement failed to hit on an exchange-rate structure that would restore monetary equilibrium in the demand and supply for different currencies. With inflation raging at different rates in different countries, that was doubtless impossible. The Nixon Administration, in any case, made virtually no effort to defend the Smithsonian exchange rates. It practiced the doctrine of "benign neglect," secure in the belief that foreigners had no alternative to taking in more dollars unless they would be willing to further increase the value of their own currencies, which the United States still wanted them to do.

The impact of the devaluation of the dollar on domestic inflation in the United States caught Washington and most economists by surprise. American economists tended to minimize the importance of foreign trade to the United States, since exports or imports constitute a seemingly small part (only 7 percent) of this country's Gross National Product. But the dollar devaluation, combined with expansive fiscal and monetary policy, intensified inflationary pressures, which wage and price controls could barely suppress.

Devaluation spurred domestic inflation in the United States, certainly in the short run, by raising the dollar prices here of internationally traded goods—not only the prices of imports entering the United States but also, and more important, the prices of all exportable American goods as well. Many American products suddenly looked like a terrific bargain to foreigners, and they rushed to buy—beef in Chicago, oil in Baton Rouge, oil paintings at Sotheby Parke-Bernet Galleries in New York, real estate in Houston, and farmland in Iowa. The effect of devaluation was immediate on primary products, such as food and raw materials, but more gradual on the prices of manufactured goods such as automobiles and tractors, especially under then-existing price controls. But as the prices of such basic internationally traded raw-material "inputs" as iron and steel, copper, aluminum, zinc, lead, and plastics rose, so did the prices of autos, tractors, and other manufactured goods. And when President Nixon's price controls were lifted, the prices of industrial goods soared.

Ironically, the devaluation of the dollar initially had a perverse effect on the United States balance of trade and payments. Economists had expected some lag, but it lasted longer than it was supposed to. Indeed, the dollar outflow quickened. The reason was that the devaluation increased the dollar price of imports—especially because of the high income-elasticity of the American demand for imports. The American economy, driven forward by expansive fiscal and monetary policies, was expanding more rapidly and sucking in more goods from abroad.

Simultaneously, devaluation cut the dollar price of American exports, causing foreign demand for cheaper American goods to boom. To check the outflow of certain goods, the United States imposed export controls on soybeans and other agricultural goods—greatly upsetting the Japanese in particular and restricting the rise of American earnings abroad. Even more important, booming demand at home restricted the growth of United States exports. Hence the American trade position worsened, and dollars continued to flow overseas to cover the payments gap.

The basic United States blunder was to think it could run a noninflationary devaluation of the dollar without first slowing the economy. It did just the reverse—coupling devaluation with strong fiscal and monetary stimulus.

A Floating World Monetary System

The fixed-exchange rate system could not survive the continuing dollar outflow. In early 1973 there was a second dollar devaluation, amounting to 10 percent, following a dramatic around-the-world flight by then Under Secretary of the Treasury, Paul Volcker (later the president of the Federal Reserve Bank of New York). But instead of calming the foreign-exchange markets, it roiled them further.

In late February and early March, dollars began to flood into West Germany because the mark looked like the safest port in a storm. The German central bank took in over $3 billion a day, paying out marks to all comers in a vain attempt to keep the mark's value from rising. After dishing out more than $10 billion worth of marks, German monetary officials at the Bundesbank (West Germany's Federal Reserve System) grew frightened of the inflation they would cause if they kept taking in masses of dollars from abroad and paying out marks. They threw in the sponge—stopped defending the fixed exchange rate between the dollar and the mark; so the mark floated upward, and the dollar floated downward.

The Bretton Woods fixed-rate system was dead; the whole world monetary system was afloat, with currencies moving up or down in response to the supply and demand for each currency. The Western European nations, striving for monetary and economic integration, tried to hold their currencies inside a "snake"—really a water snake, which floated about in relation to the dollar.

World Inflation

The loss of respect for the dollar, the key currency of the world monetary system, brought on a flight from all currencies into anything precious and scarce that would hold its value in a time of monetary crisis—gold, silver, platinum, and many other commodities, all of which seemed suddenly in short supply—as demand raced ahead of supply at existing prices, and prices soared. Overnight it seemed as though the gloomy long-range forecasts of the exhaustion of world resources were coming true in a rush, with world inflation the fever gauge of commodity shortages.

Accidents of nature fed the commodity inflation. One of the weirdest was the disappearance of anchovies off the coast of Peru. Why this happened is still unclear. One theory is that the cause was the 1972–73 invasion of a warm-water current called *El Niño*, which upset the ecology of the cold-water Humboldt Current, drastically reducing the supply of plankton and other nutrients on which anchovies (as well as whales) feed. Some marine biologists, however, doubt that this was the cause, pointing out that El Niño had arrived in 1957 and again in 1962—but had not earlier seriously damaged the anchovy stock. Did an influx of predators eat the spawn? Were the young fish blown into hostile waters? Nobody really knows what micro-factor reduced the supply of anchovies. Whatever the explanation, as the Morgan Guaranty Bank's economists stressed, Peru's anchovy catch fell from more than 10 million tons to 2 million tons in 1973, wiping out a critical part of the world's fishmeal supply, which is used to feed livestock. The markets for cattle, pigs, and anchovies are interdependent.

Bad growing weather for cereals, the failure of much of the Soviet Union's grain crop, the massive Soviet-American wheat deal—a key element in the politics of détente—all exacerbated the commodity inflation.

But the overall inflationary trend was no fluke, not a result of a series of micro-accidents. All nations were in a simultaneous economic boom, and the world's aggregate demand was outrunning aggregate supply. The vast outflow of U.S. dollars had more than doubled world monetary reserves and was a major cause of world inflation. The public's perception of rising prices was transmogrified, as inevitably happens when an inflation lasts long enough, into a perception that paper money was losing its value and was not worth holding. Speculators rushed from currencies into commodities. By October of 1973, world commodity prices had more than doubled from the start of the year.

And then, with the outbreak of the Yom Kippur war in the Middle East, the Arabs launched their oil weapon against the West.

The Oil Explosion

World commodity inflation had given the oil producers both the motivation and the opportunity to boost their prices sky-high. The rising cost of imports to the Arabs, Iranians, and other oil-producing states, the rapidly growing demand for oil, thanks to the simultaneous boom in all the major industrial countries, the disappearance of American buffer stocks of oil—all these developments gave OPEC the golden opportunity for a financial killing.

The Arab oil embargo, designed to induce the Western powers to force Israel to yield to Arab demands, cut the world oil supply at the critical moment, threw the Western allies into disarray in a mad scramble for oil, and paved the way for a fourfold increase in the price of crude oil. The price in the Persian Gulf was jacked up from about $2.10 a barrel to $8 a barrel. That meant the greatest single financial coup in history—a $70 billion haul by the oil producers in a single year. Arab nations will continue to reap enormous income from oil year after year until the world's oil importers cut their oil consumption or develop energy supplies of their own—or until the oil producers run out of oil.

The fantastic transfer of money to the oil-producing countries created an unprecedented shock for the world economy. That shock was, paradoxically, both inflationary and contractionary.

The huge increase in oil prices and payments worsened inflation in the United States, Japan, and Western Europe by increasing both living costs and costs of production. It put powerful pressure, both direct and indirect, upon the industrial and the developing countries to increase their export prices in order to cover their oil deficits. To be sure, high prices are bringing out more oil and helping to restrain the growth of demand. And high prices for oil are also providing impetus to the development of alternative sources of energy—coal, nuclear, and solar. This will over time erode the power of OPEC. But when? The crystal ball fogs over.

The Threat to Trade

Meanwhile, however, the enormous transfer of funds to the oil producers has retarded consumption and productive investment in the West, exacerbating the problem of stagflation. It is as though OPEC had levied an annual tax of $100 billion a year upon the rest of the world. Such a tax increase, as macroeconomics teaches us, will have a contractionary effect on national economies unless the money collected is put back into the economies from which it is collected in the form of expenditures on consumer goods or capital goods.

If the major share of "oil taxes" collected by foreign governments is not re-spent or reinvested in production, it will choke off output and income in the oil-importing countries.

The danger is that the world economy, in the midst of chronic inflation, payments deficits, and unemployment, could slide back into protectionism and beggar-my-neighbor policies that would worsen a world slump—with potentially disastrous political consequences.

CHAPTER EIGHT
Economics in Action: Government

Economic logic must always be subject to the test of what happens in the real world. It was the eighteenth-century philosopher David Hume—also a pioneer of economics— who showed in his *Treatise of Human Nature* that the truths of reason are true by definition but that the truths of the world we live in are based on experience, not abstract logic.[1]

So it is essential that we look at actual cases of economics in action, if we are to establish economic truths. Take, for instance, the matter we just mentioned at the close of the last chapter: the economic and political consequences of protectionism. Let us examine what happened in 1930 when

Congress passed the highly protectionist Hawley-Smoot Tariff Act.

As though to disprove the old saw that if all economists were laid end to end they would never reach a conclusion, 1,038 American economists—including virtually every reputable economist in the country of whatever political view—signed a petition urging President Herbert Hoover to veto the bill. The economists warned that if enacted Hawley-Smoot would "inevitably provoke other countries to pay us back in kind"—with damaging impact on the United States as well as other nations.

But President Hoover ignored the economists' advice. The Republican Party had traditionally favored high tariff policies as a formula for economic prosperity. And the Republican platform of 1928 had promised to relieve the already present depression in agriculture by raising tariff rates on farm products.

Soon after taking office in January of 1929, President Hoover, determined to keep his party's promise to the farmers, called together a special session of Congress. By June, the House of Representatives reported to the floor a tariff bill in substantially the form recommended by the President. But then the process of logrolling and what is now called "Christmas-treeing" began; a great many amendments were added to the bill, raising tariff rates across the entire range of imports.

The politically appetizing process of increasing tariff rates and extending coverage to other products continued in the Senate. The Senate-House conference committee generally compromised by accepting the highest rates set by either house. When the bill reached President Hoover, he signed it because, as Professor Frank Taussig of Harvard, a distinguished economist of the day, wrote, "His party could not go before the country stultified by having nothing whatever to show for a year's prolonged and conspicuous labor."

With business slumping, opposition to foreign firms' entering the American market mounted. Some of the more important pressure groups traditionally in favor of liberal trade had not maintained firm and unyielding opposition to the Hawley-Smoot bill. Labor realized that higher prices would result, but succumbed to the hope that the bill would relieve unemployment, which was already rising seriously, by stimulating domestic output of goods to replace imports. Farmers were willing to grasp at any protection that might possibly help them, despite their need for foreign markets.

The economists proved right in their warning of the likelihood of foreign retaliation. France, Italy, Spain, and others raised tariff barriers or introduced drastic quotas on imports in 1930. Switzerland initiated a largely successful boycott of American products. Canada raised its tariff walls to the highest point in its history. Great Britain passed the Emergency Tariff Act of 1931 and the Import Duties Act of 1932. The British Commonwealth concluded severely discriminatory preferential tariff arrangements in Ottawa in 1932.

The higher trade barriers of the United States frustrated the efforts of the Japanese government to improve economic conditions through expanded trade and led to a more nationalistic and militant foreign policy. Hawley-Smoot sowed the seeds of the Japanese Asian Co-Prosperity Sphere. International conferences to work out a truce in the trade war failed in 1931, 1932, and 1933.

The United States was worse off after Hawley-Smoot than it had been before. Other countries raised their tariffs and other trade barriers even more than we did. American exports sank like a stone—because of both the higher trade barriers and the spreading world depression, to which the collapse of trade contributed.

By 1932, United States exports to Great Britain had fallen to *one third of their 1929 level.* In 1932, American exports to Canada and France were only *one fourth of 1929,* and, in the case of Australia and Oceania, *one fifth of 1929.*

The decline of some specific American export commodities was even more dramatic. Agriculture, the sector that the President had originally sought to benefit, suffered most. Wheat exports, which had totaled $200 million ten years earlier, fell to $5 million in 1932. Exports of the automobile industry fell from $541 million in 1929 to $76 million in 1932.

In retrospect, the protectionist Hawley-Smoot Act was worse than futile. It did not solve unemployment or other problems of American labor, industry, and agriculture; instead, it worsened them by helping to shatter world trade. Its repercussions contributed to the growth of nationalism in many countries and to the deepening political and economic crisis of the 1930's. It helped bring on the Second World War in Europe and Asia.

Profiting from the Lesson in International Economics

The United States and other Western countries presumably learned the lessons of Hawley-Smoot and the protectionism that followed in its train. The American leadership in post-World War II reconstruction put heavy stress on continuous progress toward a liberal world trading system.

But by the summer of 1977, in the wake of the severe world recession and inflation, the International Monetary

Fund warned that there had been a serious break in the pattern of trade and payments liberalization that had marked world economic policy of the three decades after the war. The IMF found that, despite their pledges to free trade, more and more countries were adopting "restrictive policies —especially nontariff barriers to imports, which were supported to an increasing extent by the negotiation of export restraint agreements." A nontariff barrier (or NTB) can be any of a wide variety of obstacles to foreign trade, including quotas on imports, "buy American" or "buy British" legislation, health and safety regulations, bureaucratic red tape, or other barriers to foreign countries' goods.

The pressures of high unemployment and massive imbalances in nations' payment deficits had encroached on the principles of liberalization. The United States set quotas on most types of specialty steel and then imposed quotas on imports of beef, veal, and mutton. France, West Germany, and Britain restricted imports of textiles and garments from developing countries. Japan subjected imports of silk yarn to prior notification and entered into an export restraint agreement with Korea on silk yarns. Brazil tightened import controls and suspended imports of many items. Peru set up a system of restrictive import licensing. Even some oil-rich— but spendthrift—countries, such as Iran and Nigeria, have had to clamp on import controls.

Thus, Adam Smith's principle of free trade is once again in jeopardy, as it always is when business slump and unemployment afflict the world. Is free trade a fair-weather system? Maybe so. But protectionism is no solution; it is only an aggravant of a worldwide slump.

The hard job of knowledgeable politicians is to contain or appease the pressures of the special interests for protection against foreign competition—but without wrecking liberal international trade. The political and military, as well as the economic, costs of protectionism may be unbearable. Beggar-thy-neighbor economics ultimately means beggar thyself.

Why Governments Create Inflation: After the French Revolution

The task facing governments, that of creating enough aggregate demand to cure a slump and unemployment, but not so much as to cause inflation, sounds modern, but it is centuries old. Take what happened during the French Revolution.

The French Revolution of 1789 began, of course, as a reaction against the extravagant, lascivious, pleasure-loving habits of the aristocrats. For a brief time after the revolution, simple spartan values prevailed in the new republic. But, because the revolution had frightened business and driven capital and gold out of the country or into hiding, business and trade stagnated.

To cure this stagnation, the Revolutionary government of France began in 1790 to print paper money, the so-called "assignats." These were issued against the security of the vast public lands confiscated from the church and the emigrant noblemen. The assignats were also designed to help the common people acquire these public lands and thus change the social order.

At first the issue of assignats worked beautifully and did exactly what it was supposed to do—stimulate production, revive employment, and get the country humming again. But this initial success generated demands for more of the same treatment, and the new government could not find the courage to stop issuing paper money in time—before it had set a genuine inflation in motion. As more and more assignats poured from the printing presses, prices climbed, and a new disease in the character of the French people began to spread.

One of the symptoms of this new social disease was the obliteration of thrift. A celebrated historian of the decay, Andrew Dickson White, whose *Fiat Money Inflation in France* (1876)[2] is a minor classic, noted: "The French are naturally thrifty, but, with such masses of money and with such uncertainty as to its future value, the ordinary motives for saving and care diminished, and a loose luxury spread throughout the country."

Speculation and gambling became epidemic. Some gamblers rushed to the stock market, others to the roulette wheel. Throughout the country, a deep dislike for steady labor set in. Workers loafed and businessmen saw no point in going after moderate gains through hard work, steady investment, and step-by-step technical improvements.

A new reckless spirit spread to official circles. Even heroes of the Revolution such as Mirabeau became cynical and corrupt and began to take heavy bribes while still mouthing the rhetoric of popular reform. The disease spread even to journalism, where it took deep and lasting root. As Andrew White observed, the corruption stemming from inflation "grew as naturally as a fungus on a muck heap." At the start of the revolution, the leading women in French society showed a nobility of character and a simplicity of dress worthy of Roman matrons; "but now all was changed," said

White. "At the head of society stood Madame Tallien and others like her, wild in extravagance, daily seeking new refinements in luxury, and demanding of their husbands and lovers vast sums to array them and to feed their whims."

The inflation had bred a class of people with a vested interest in more inflation. People who had contracted large debts had a powerful motive for wanting the value of money to continue to cheapen so that they could pay off their debts in depreciated francs. Speculators had a vital interest in the continuing rise of prices. All business had become a game of chance, said White, and all businessmen, gamblers.

Here is what had happened to prices in France, according to a table published in mid-1795, which White reduced to American coinage (in terms of U.S. prices in 1876):

	1790	1795
For a bushel of flour	40¢	$45
For a bushel of oats	18¢	$10
For a cartload of wood	$4	$500
For a pound of soap	18¢	$8
For a pair of shoes	$1	$40

Businessmen had at first thought of themselves as pure beneficiaries of inflation; they were happy to see the value of goods on their shelves or in warehouses bid up by people holding a plethora of assignats. But they soon found that, as they put up prices, buying began to lag, and payments became less sure. Their own costs were shooting up. A sense of insecurity spread; enterprise was deadened. And the French economy slumped.

Almost two centuries later, the post-French Revolution episode had a fascinating reprise. It happened on the New Frontier and in the Great Society of Washington.

... The New Economics and Vietnam

The economists that President John F. Kennedy brought to Washington in 1961 were all disciples of John Maynard Keynes. They firmly believed that managing aggregate demand would enable the government to reduce unemployment and, if it should occur, inflation. But it was unemployment that the Kennedy Administration regarded as the nation's immediate economic problem; and to that problem Mr. Kennedy's top economists—Walter W. Heller, Kermit Gordon, and James Tobin—applied standard Keynesian remedies to bolster aggregate demand.

There were differences within the Kennedy Administration on how to strengthen demand. Ambassador John Kenneth Galbraith, from his outpost in New Delhi, kept urging greater emphasis on social spending programs, which he saw as a means of using one stone to kill two birds, unemployment and public squalor. But the President's Council of Economic Advisers put greater emphasis on tax cuts to boost aggregate demand on practical, political grounds. They were perfectly willing to support enlarged public spending, but thought that the amounts the President could extract from a reluctant Congress would be too small to cure unemployment and get the economy moving fast enough.

President Kennedy himself was, however, reluctant to call for major tax reduction at first; a major theme in his electoral campaign had been a call for national sacrifice—"Ask not what your country can do for you, but what you can do for your country"—and accepting a tax cut didn't seem like asking people to do very much. However, with Chairman Walter Heller of the Council of Economic Advisers waging an effective educational campaign for tax reduction both inside and outside the Administration, the President gradually came around and started to campaign for a massive tax cut.

President Kennedy was assassinated before he could get Congress to enact the tax cut. It was President Lyndon B. Johnson who swiftly pushed the tax cut through Congress in early 1964. Although it is certainly easier to get a tax cut than a tax increase through the legislature, Congress was reluctant to approve a tax cut of over $10 billion—at a time when the Federal budget was already running $10 billion in the red. As Walter Heller remarked, the nation was still dominated by the "Puritan ethic," which, in fiscal matters, meant "Balance the budget, stay out of debt, live within your means." The tax cut, said Mr. Heller, would help *close* the budget gap, not widen it, because it would raise national output, national income, and therefore the tax yield to the Federal government.

Under pressure from LBJ, Congress bought the concept and voted for a big tax reduction while the budget was still deep in deficit. This represented the triumph of an idea; as Keynes said, "The ideas of economists and political philosophers, both when they are right and when they are wrong, are more powerful than is commonly understood." But they are far from omnipotent, as was soon to be demonstrated. Indeed, in the short run, it is the politicians who call the tune.

The economy responded vigorously to the big tax cut—it was worth $14 billion to taxpayers—just as the Keynesians, now called the "New Economists," said it would: national economic output surged forward, unemployment declined, and the gap in the Federal budget narrowed—as rising national income threw off higher tax payments. The miracle had worked, and the prestige of Keynesian doctrine—and of the New Economists—soared to a historic high.

By the end of 1965, unemployment had fallen to 4 percent of the labor force—the level that Walter Heller had at first called the "full employment" target and later, under political criticism, had relabeled an "interim target." But, with unemployment down to 4 percent and still declining, prices began to rise. President Johnson's economic advisers—by then Gardner Ackley had succeeded Walter Heller as chairman of the Council of Economic Advisers, and the Council's other two members were Otto Eckstein and Arthur Okun—now wanted economic policy gradually reversed, that is, switched from stimulus to restraint. In accordance with the New Economics, which they saw as symmetrical, they began to urge an *increase* in taxes, rather than a tax cut. They feared that the President's decision to escalate the war in Vietnam might, by rapidly raising defense expenditures, overburden an already fully employed economy. LBJ would not allow his economists to "go public" with their campaign for a tax increase; they carried it on cautiously, nervously, within the Administration.

But the President was unwilling to accept his economists' advice; instead, he decided to go for a "guns *and* butter" economic policy, hoping to pay for what still seemed like a relatively small war in Vietnam with the extra resources flowing from an expanding economy. LBJ apparently chose this course for two major reasons: to avoid a raucous debate in Congress over Vietnam and to avoid having a Congress that did not want to raise taxes deny him the Great Society anti-poverty and other social programs he sought as the positive contribution that would give him his place in history beside Franklin D. Roosevelt as a friend of the "forgotten man."

President Johnson's hope that he could find the extra resources to deal with the nation's military and social needs without a tax increase, and without inflation, failed. By the middle of the summer of 1966 the Administration was battling to prevent the complete collapse of its economic policy.

Successive blows—first by labor, then by industry—left the Administration's wage-price guideposts to contain inflation so battered that they could not be salvaged. The airline machinists overwhelmingly rejected the settlement their leaders had worked out in the White House with Johnson himself. And the Inland Steel Corporation—which once had helped beat down a steel industry price increase during the Kennedy Administration—announced a price increase that the rest of the industry quickly followed. President Johnson's unwillingness to use fiscal policy in the form of a tax increase had put unbearable pressure on the wage-price guideposts.

When inflation began to speed up in 1966 and 1967, it proved harder than LBJ or his economists had expected to turn policy toward restraint. Congress and the nation resisted a tax increase, and the President did not want a public defeat. Finally, in August 1967, President Johnson asked Congress for the tax increase his economists had long counseled —but he did not get it until the summer of 1968. By then the boom and inflation were out of the bag, and inflationary expectations were so strong that the 10 percent surtax on personal and corporate income had less effect than expected.

So war, inflation, and the long-delayed tax hike sealed the doom of LBJ and the Democrats. It also badly hurt the reputation of the New Economists. In 1968 and 1969 their stock fell far below the peak it had reached in 1964 with the highly effective $14 billion tax cut. Politics had triumphed over economics—and the economists. But it was a Pyrrhic victory, and President Johnson expired of a self-inflicted wound.

The New, New Economics—and Nixonomics

Thus, as unemployment was the Number One problem faced by John F. Kennedy when he reached the White House in 1961, so inflation was the nation's primary problem when Richard M. Nixon took office in January 1969.

Nixon had been counseled on economic policy during his campaign by Professor Milton Friedman of the University of Chicago and several of his monetarist disciples or sympathizers. Professor Friedman had been trying for some years to stage a counterrevolution against the Keynesian Revolution, which he criticized for its relative neglect and downgrading of *monetary* policy, for its overstress on fiscal policy, and for its endorsement of so much government interference in the private economy.

The economists that President Nixon named to his Council of Economic Advisers—Chairman Paul McCracken, Hendrik Houthakker, and Herbert Stein—had been much influenced by Friedman's theory that gradual growth in the money supply would check inflation without causing a recession or much rise in unemployment. Friedman himself preferred to stay outside Washington and at his academic post, though he remained influential.

A test of Friedman's "new, new economics" was now to

be made, to stop the inflation. In his book *Capitalism and Freedom,* Friedman had put the formula very succinctly: "I would specify that the reserve system shall see to it that the total stock of money . . . rises month by month, and indeed, so far as possible, day by day, at an annual rate of X percent, where X is some number between 3 and 5." The reason for his choosing a money-supply growth rate between those two numbers is that the United States economy's long-term growth rate lies between 3 and 5 percent per year. Friedman dismissed the complications of which definition of the money supply to use—there are at least ten,* according to the calculation of Henry C. Wallich, a member of the Federal Reserve Board—or precisely what numerical growth rate to follow, saying that these make "far less difference than the definite choice of a particular definition and a particular rate of growth."[3]

Friedman's theory obviously had strong appeal to an Administration that did not want to increase taxes as a means of stopping inflation—and that in any case regarded Johnson's tax increase as a failure. Friedman's theory was also attractive to Nixon in that it did not require the Administration to intervene in the wage and price decisions of labor and business—Nixon was particularly anxious not to offend business as the Kennedy and Johnson Administrations had done. The Friedman theory asserted that such government intervention would only distort the use of resources, be unfair to particular companies, industries, or workers, and would in any case have no effect whatsoever on inflation,

---

* But the two principal ones are M-1—currency in circulation plus demand deposits; and M-2—currency in circulation and demand deposits plus time and savings deposits, as indicated on pages 87–8.

this being a result of too rapid an increase in the money supply.

During President Nixon's first year in office, the money supply—defined as demand deposits plus currency in circulation—was held down to a rate of growth of only 2½ percent. But consumer prices climbed at an annual rate of about 6 percent until the second half of 1970, when the inflation rate slowed to about 4½ percent. But in the first half of 1971 the inflation appeared to be picking up again.

On the other side, with the slowdown in the money supply, the economy had gone into recession and unemployment had gone up from 3½ percent to over 6 percent of the labor force. President Nixon and his economic advisers said that they would use the concept of a "full-employment budget"— one in which revenues would equal expenditures only if the economy were at full employment, while accepting sizable deficits if the economy were well below full-capacity use. Nixon's economists clearly did not like to have their fiscal policy branded "liberal." Herbert Stein, who had provided an early post-World War II formulation of the full-employment budget, insisted that the doctrine had a good, conservative, Republican lineage.

At the same time, Nixon's economists now sought to persuade the Federal Reserve Board, under the chairmanship of Arthur F. Burns, Nixon's appointee, to increase the rate of growth of the money supply faster than the Friedman formula of 3 to 5 percent called for—or than Dr. Burns himself thought prudent. The President's Council of Economic Advisers maintained that monetary growth at a rate of more than 6 percent—perhaps as much as 9 percent—was essential to restore full employment by the end of 1972. And the

Council denied that so rapid a rate of monetary growth, if it were not continued too long, would reactivate inflation.

To buy a little extra anti-inflationary insurance, the Nixon Administration began to shift away from its strong opposition to wage and price restraints and to adopt, though somewhat reluctantly, an "incomes policy." As an Administration spokesman put it: "In order to help assure that the inflation rate moves down as the real economy moves up, the Administration has become increasingly active in using its influence to restrain directly price and wage increases in particular industries."

The cautious steps taken, however, were not enough to satisfy Chairman Burns of the Federal Reserve Board, the Administration's most important critic—most important because he controlled the money supply. In March 1971, Dr. Burns told the Senate Banking and Currency Committee: "I don't think our fiscal and monetary policies are sufficient to control inflation," and again urged the Nixon Administration to establish the type of wage and price review board that he then regarded as central to an effective incomes policy. The findings of such a board, said Burns, could be used not only to create a case-law basis for wage-price guidelines but also to support the President's efforts to deal with inflationary actions by labor or industry. Walter Heller, Gardner Ackley, Arthur Okun and other Kennedy-Johnson economists could not have agreed more.

But President Nixon was furious with Burns for hectoring and pressuring him. He unleashed Charles Colson to launch a flank attack on Burns via the press. But the banking and business reaction in support of Burns caused Nixon quickly to back off.

Then suddenly—on August 15, 1971—Nixon froze wages

and prices, following the advice of Secretary of the Treasury John B. Connally. The adoption of controls staggered Nixon's free-enterprise economists—including Milton Friedman at his redoubt at the University of Chicago. They quickly adjusted, rationalizing the President's move as having been forced upon him by the Democrats and the Eastern Establishment press, especially *The New York Times.*

Politics had again triumphed over economics—and the economists licked their wounds and made the best of it. Only this time the wounded economists were Nixon conservatives and Friedmanians, not LBJ liberals and Keynesians.

The Many Faces of Communism

In the Communist world, economics—and economic systems —also are shaped by the visible hands of political leaders. At the end of the Nixon Administration, when the war in Southeast Asia was finally closed out, the Communist regimes in Vietnam and Cambodia appeared to be headed in opposite directions.

South Vietnam, though joined to North Vietnam, was planning an economy more market-oriented, with more scope for private business, than North Vietnam's planned economy. Meanwhile, Cambodia had moved to create a national economy so totally communized that it would entail the abolition of money, the payment of wages, and all private ownership of property—even of private plots of land by peasants.

Which nation, South Vietnam or Cambodia, was the straw in the wind telling which way Communism would be blowing in Asia? It certainly did not seem to be Cambodia, whose rural revolutionary leaders were taking the country back to the Middle Ages. Cambodia's cities were ruthlessly drained of their populations. Phnom Penh, at its wartime peak a city of two and a half million, became a ghost town of empty streets, patrolled by armed security men.

The liquidation of the cities of Cambodia represented in part a response by the revolutionary leaders to the danger of mass starvation, with the cutting of the transport of food supplies up the Mekong River. The urban population was driven by the Communists back to the land to help raise rice.

But the forced return to the land of the city dwellers appears to have been based not just on practical economics but on strong emotional factors as well. There was a clear hatred among the rural revolutionaries of all Western things, and the cities were associated with venality and corruption.

It is difficult to say whether Cambodia's leaders will seek to keep their country rural and backward indefinitely or whether the present scheme is simply the result of immediate necessity and anger. They are, however, thinking of some degree of international trade, and, to trade abroad, Cambodia is going to have to raise production above the subsistence needs of its own population. Cambodia's extreme form of Communism is thus likely to be an expedient that will moderate when the nation gets through the crucial transition period from war to peace and when the fury of the rural revolutionaries dies down.

Ironically, South Vietnam's more capitalistic variety of Communism also can be explained as a consequence of that nation's struggle to survive after the departure of the American army and business organizations. South Vietnam's brand of Communism also stems from its more urban social structure, the heavier capitalization of its industry, its dependence

on foreign trade, and the different—and more sophisticated
—character of its political leaders.

After the Americans left Vietnam, unemployment was
enormous; somewhere between one third and one fourth of
the labor force was left jobless. The Communist leaders, fearing a total economic collapse, sought foreign aid from the
United States as well as other countries. And South Vietnam's leaders decided to build a "mixed economy" divided
into private and public sectors.

An "individual" (private) sector would include small
shops and personal services. Another private sector would
include some factories remaining in the hands of what is
called the "national bourgeoisie," or even of foreign owners,
who would be permitted to make "adequate profits."

Peasants would be allowed to keep their land and farm it,
but the state would have a monopoly of rice buying and
selling. There would also be a "collective" sector, presumably in agriculture as well as industry, but workers' participa-
tion in this would depend on "self-willingness."

South Vietnam's leaders apparently felt that they lacked
the capital, technological know-how, and management cadres
to operate a more advanced socialist system, and hence were
adopting a program to keep the economy viable for the immediate years ahead. This would follow the example of
what Soviet leaders did after the Russian Revolution when
the economy was a shambles. Under the so-called New Economic Policy (NEP), which was launched in 1921 and which
lasted until the first five-year plan of 1928, private trade
was permitted to develop because the job of collectivizing
industry, trade, and agriculture was too great for the Communist party. Lenin called NEP "a step backward in order

the better to leap forward." Stalin eventually collectivized agriculture, got rid of the small landholders and entrepreneurs, and buried NEP.

Is South Vietnam likely to run this course? Asked whether the new mixed economy in South Vietnam was seen as a permanent system or merely a transitional step toward fuller socialism, Mrs. Nguyen Thi Binh, a high-ranking member of Saigon's Provisional Revolutionary Government, replied: "We hold this policy as a long-range one."

Clearly, Communism is no monolith. The first great schism in the Communist "church" occurred when Mao Tse-tung broke with Marxism-Leninism-Stalinism as preached in Moscow. The Maoist vision was of a truly honest, simple, modest, and classless society—not one dominated by a "new class" of self-rewarding bureaucrats and superproletarians.

Communism, said Mao, would go through many different phases, experience many revolutions. As Professor John Gurley of Stanford University, a close and sympathetic student of Maoist economics, has observed, Mao did not see Communism as the last stage of world development. Indeed, Mao did not see human beings as the final stage of the development of life on earth, but held forth the secular and messianic vision of higher forms of life to come when mankind has died out.

"Mankind will eventually reach its doomsday," Mao prophesied. "When theologians talk about doomsday, it is pessimism used to scare people. When we speak about the destruction of mankind, we are saying that something more advanced than mankind will be produced."

Thus the dialectics of destruction-construction remain Mao's legacy to China's new leaders, who may set the nation on a more pragmatic course of industrialism and economic development. But, in the twentieth century and still close to the "beginning" of the revolution, China's leaders still believe in the necessity of the state and party as the "vanguard" of their own nation and of the human race. The concept of the dictatorship of the proletariat has not disappeared, or been seriously weakened, despite the great schism between China and the Soviet Union.

But are we now witnessing in Western Europe another major schism in Communism, with a genuine departure from the concept of the dictatorship of the proletariat?

The Communist parties of Italy, France, and Spain are in the forefront of the new European political movement dubbed "Eurocommunism." Enrico Berlinguer, leader of the Italian Communist party, has proclaimed its commitment to democracy and to civil liberties, and in effect to the reversibility of Communist accession to power if the people so decide in free elections.

Will Rome or Paris or Madrid become the center of alternative Communist ideologies to those of Moscow and Peking? Berlinguer and Georges Marchais, leader of the hitherto Stalinist Communist party of France, have declared their parties' joint commitment to "liberty of thought and expression, of press, of meeting and association, the right to demonstrate, to travel in and out of the country, the inviolability of private life, religious freedom, total freedom to express diverse ideologies and philosophical, cultural, and artistic opinion."

There are reasons for skepticism whether Communists will remain democrats and protectors of freedom once they attain power—and whether their declaration of democratic principles is not simply a ruse to pave their way to power among peoples committed to democracy, after which the

Communists' democratic principles will be jettisoned. Their failure to criticize Moscow on human rights issues provokes suspicion.

Nevertheless, whatever their sincerity or insincerity, such declarations focus attention on the greatest weakness in Communist systems as they exist in all nations where Communists have actually come to power: the leaders' lack of accountability to the people and the sacrifice of freedom to an alleged commitment to social and economic equality.

Equality and/or Freedom

Are equality and freedom incompatible?

Capitalist societies have thus far failed to combine social and economic equality with the personal and political freedoms that have been the proudest achievement of the "great bourgeois democratic revolutions."

Enormous disparities persist in wealth and income within the capitalist countries. The huge increase in total wealth of capitalist societies, far from ending the issue of equality, has intensified it—by removing much of the justification for wide income disparities as the necessary condition for high capital formation and economic growth.

In the United States, the struggle over greater equality takes many forms, not only over wages and income but over how to reform the tax laws, the welfare system, health services, and how to provide more equal access for people of different races and sexes to jobs, education, and housing. A new aspect of this issue is how to rescue the decaying cities engulfed by the poor and the desperate, including a high proportion of young people who have never had a regular job.

CHAPTER NINE

Economics in Action: Business

In capitalist economies, individual businessmen make the big decisions: what to produce; how to produce it; how much to pay for labor, materials, land, patents; how much to charge for products; whether to produce at home, to import, or produce abroad; whether to try to develop new technology; how much and when to invest in new plant and equipment, etc., etc. All such decisions are subject to market constraints and political pressures—as the following examples show.

Price Competition in the Air

Southwest Airlines was organized in 1967 to provide service between Houston, Dallas/Fort Worth, and San Antonio. Since its flights would be entirely within the state of Texas, Southwest Airlines did not have to apply for a license to the Civil Aeronautics Board, which regulates only interstate air transportation. Southwest got its certificate from the Texas Aeronautics Commission in 1968.

Immediately afterward, Braniff and Texas International, two interstate airlines already serving the three Texas cities, sought an injunction to prevent Southwest from operating; Braniff and TI obviously did not welcome the local competition, free of CAB control. For three years, Southwest Airlines fought in the courts and finally won its right to operate from the U.S. Supreme Court.

Once in operation, Southwest lowered the fare on all three routes from $27 to $20. It also began an extensive advertising campaign featuring hostesses dressed in hot pants, cut-rate and exotically named $1 drinks ("love potions for the very weary"), and fast ticketing. Southwest issued preprinted tickets, recording passengers' names on a foot-operated tape recorder. Its overall advertising theme was "At last there's someone up there who loves you."

Braniff and Texas International moved to meet this challenge. Braniff cuts its fares to $20 and started advertising "every-hour-on-the-hour" service and such extras as hot towels and free "peace of mind" telephone calls from the check-in gate. TI offered free beer, free newspapers, and $1 drinks on the three Texas routes that Southwest flew.

Undaunted, Southwest replied with ads that said, "Other airlines may have met our price, but you can't buy love." In a curious mixture of sexism and antisexism, Southwest said of its typical hostess: "She will not plee-aze you. Plee-aze is stiff, formal and very affected English for please. It is usually accompanied by a gleaming toothpaste smile. People who say plee-aze are trying very, very hard to be nice to you. Too hard ..." This was presumably also a slam at Braniff's and TI's hostesses.

When a consumer survey revealed that Houston passengers would prefer using Hobby Airport (12 miles southeast of the city) instead of Houston International Airport (26 miles away), Southwest switched all of its flights to Hobby. Braniff followed suit.

Southwest offered a bargain fare of $10 on Friday nights after 9 P.M. (the marginal cost of carrying an extra passenger on a mostly empty plane is close to zero) and sent out coupons good for one trial "free ride" to 25,000 executives (also a low-cost promotion when extra seats are available). They also sent a mailing to executive secretaries, offering a "sweetheart stamp" for each flight a secretary booked for her boss on Southwest. For every fifteen stamps, a secretary won a free ride for herself.

A year later, however, Southwest, driving for a larger share of the market, had accumulated a $3.75 million deficit and was forced to raise its rate back to $26. Braniff and TI immediately raised their prices as well, hoping that the rogue competitor had been brought to heel, and still might be knocked off altogether.

In February of 1973, Braniff announced a 60-day "get acquainted" half-price fare on all flights between Dallas and Houston's Hobby Airport; the offer was not good to Houston International, since Braniff competed with Southwest only into Hobby.

Southwest countered with an angry campaign accusing Braniff of trying to force Southwest out of business, since no airline could possibly make a profit on a $13 fare. "Nobody's Going to Shoot Southwest Airlines Out of the Sky for a Lousy $13," ran its newspaper ads. Fifty thousand brochures and lapel buttons reading, "Save Love—Beat BI," were passed out in downtown Houston and Dallas by forty young women.

Southwest told customers that it would meet Braniff's $13 price if a passenger insisted on it, but urged them to pay the full $26 fare and get a free bottle of Chivas Regal Scotch whiskey instead. Many passengers chose the liquor, and Southwest became the largest distributor of Chivas Regal in the United States. Braniff finally raised its fare from $13 back to $26.

Southwest survived, and a slightly larger oligopoly (Southwest, BI, and TI) proved to be more advantageous to consumers in terms of service and price than a slightly tighter oligopoly (BI and TI).

Monopoly Profits: Taxicabs

Businessmen praise competition and love monopoly. The reason is not, as some economists have contended, that monopoly ensures a "quiet life"—it rarely does—but that it promises bigger profits.

In nearly all of America's major cities there is a tight limit on the number of taxicab licenses that can be issued. The major exception is Washington, D.C., which is so well known for its plentiful and inexpensive taxi service that a spokesman for the American Taxi Association once complained bitterly to Congress that Washington was giving the entire taxi industry "a black eye."

The taxi monopolies in other cities were implanted by businessmen who were able to get their exclusive rights legalized and enforced by municipal officials and the law courts. The drive to restrict entry into the taxicab business was spearheaded in 1929 and thereafter by the late Morris Markin, president of Checker Motors, which manufactured taxicabs. It might seem strange for an automobile manufacturer to seek to restrict entry into the taxicab business— his mass market. But by 1929 Morris Markin was also a big taxicab operator himself.

He "unified" the taxi business in New York, Chicago, Minneapolis, and Pittsburgh. And he eventually controlled, by a complex set of interlinks, Checker Taxi, Yellow Cab, Chicago Yellow Cab, Parmalee Transportation Company, Calumet Mutual Insurance Company, Benzolene Motor Fuel, and other companies.

In New York, Markin's program ran into trouble when it was discovered that Mayor James (Jimmy) Walker had accepted stock in the Parmalee Transportation Company in exchange for his promise to push for a limit on the number of taxi licenses in New York.

In Chicago, Markin moved less conspicuously. On September 25, 1929, the Chicago City Council passed an ordinance rigidly restricting taxi licenses. The story didn't even make the newspapers. Later, some Chicago aldermen claimed they never heard of the ordinance.

Back in 1929, there were 5,289 regular taxi licenses in Chicago. Three decades later there were 4,600. At the time of his death in 1970, Morris Markin and his family controlled 3,666, or 80 percent, of the 4,600 licenses authorized by the Chicago ordinance—with 1,500 of the licenses held by Checker Taxi and 2,166 by Yellow Cab, both Markin properties.

Three University of Chicago law professors, Edmund Kitch, Marc Isaacson, and Daniel Kasper, have conservatively estimated that the rate of return on invested capital for each taxicab equals 47 percent. If that rate drops, the taxicab company is entitled to a fare increase. And the existing monopoly is rigidly protected against new competition. The Chicago taxi study points up some principles that should be interesting to other monopolists—and antimonopolists:

• *Create the myth of the irresponsibility and instability of competitive conditions.* Markin and his associates played on this theme continuously. Yet Chicago had had fifty years of relative peace and convenience with both horse-drawn cabs and automobiles, with free entry and free rate setting in the taxi business—before 1929. Violence in the taxicab industry came in Chicago *after* the monopoly was established. It was caused, first by the monopolist's efforts to drive out new competition, and second, to break a strike of taxi drivers who wanted a larger percentage of the meter.

• *Bring your opponents over to your side.* Yellow and Checker made a deal with the Teamsters Union, which represented the taxi drivers. Back in the late 1930's, Dominick Abatta, a driver who was the leader of the strike, was co-opted by being made president of the Teamsters' local, and the Teamsters Union supported the taxicab companies' request for fare increases.

• *Maintain as low visibility as possible.* Let the municipal authorities play the role of mere bystander. Constantly bring cases to court—such as damage suits against the city. This stills newspaper criticism because of the papers' traditional reluctance and inability to comment critically on matters in litigation.

• *Charge high rates.* This will prevent anyone from saying that you are not providing adequate service. If prices are high enough, you can always say that there's not enough business for the existing supply of services.

• *Don't be too severe in enforcing your monopoly.* Let the gypsy cabs or jitneys operate, as long as they stay away from the most lucrative locations of the city. Your monopoly will be more secure if you don't press it too hard and arouse community sympathy for your opponents.

• *Respond to criticism.* In Chicago, for example, there was trouble over the taxi service at O'Hare Airport. The monopoly fixed this by making it more profitable for city cabs to operate at O'Hare and at the same time successfully excluded competition from suburban taxis.

The law professors' study found that "the most pernicious consequence of the monopoly ordinance has been the significant constraint imposed on the city's public transportation policy."

The Chicago taxi monopoly is under continuous pressure from gypsy cabs and others attracted by the monopoly's high profits—and inadequate services. As the Chicago Law School study observed, "A monopolist's life, even with the continuing and warm embrace of the government in power, does not seem to be a quiet one." The same observation could be made of such monopolists or ex-monopolists as the Penn Central Railroad or the New York Stock Exchange.

Media Power—and Press Freedom

To most economists, a well-functioning private market is itself a public good—a source of benefit not only to particular buyers and sellers but to the community at large. This holds for the market in ideas and information.

The First Amendment to the Constitution guarantees to the people of the United States what economists call "a free market in ideas." But some economists (as well as critics of "the media" in business and elsewhere) question how free the press really is. President Nixon, Vice President Agnew, and their aides insisted that they were attacking not press freedom but a media monopoly over the treatment of news and the formation of public opinion.

This was an extremely sensitive issue to publishers and broadcasters—especially with the President of the United States in the role of press critic. For it is government itself, as monopolist over ideas and information, that publishers, broadcasters, editorial writers, and reporters most fear. They don the mantle of John Milton, who in his *Areopagitica* of 1644 wrote: "Truth and understanding are not such wares as to be monopolized and traded in by tickets and statutes and standards. We must not think to make a staple commodity of all the knowledge in the land, to mark and license it like our broadcloth and our woolpacks."

A large part of the public apparently accepted the Nixonian charges that the press is biased and wields monopoly power. Women, blacks, and other minorities, and public-interest groups have taken up the cause, where it once was largely the province of conservatives.

But there are tough factual and policy questions to answer. To what extent do newspapers and magazines and television or radio networks and stations possess monopoly power? And, even if it should be proved that some do, what should be done about it, in the light of First Amendment protection of freedom of the press?

Professor Ronald H. Coase of the University of Chicago feels that a great deal of cant has been uttered by economists as well as by lawyers, editors, and publishers about the difference between the market for ideas and the market for goods. He contends that there is no essential difference between the two markets. "In all markets," he says, "producers have some reasons for being honest and some for being dishonest. Consumers have some information but are not fully informed or even able to digest the information they have. Regulators commonly wish to do a good job and, though often incompetent and subject to the influence of special interests, they act like this because, like all the other performers in the system, they are human beings whose strongest motives are not the highest."[1]

He contends that if the public needs protection from purveyors of bad goods and bad ideas, it probably needs the most help against bad ideas, which it is less competent to judge. Further, he adds, a good case can be made for penalizing or taxing purveyors of bad ideas because of their "negative externalities" (the harm they do society) and for rewarding purveyors of good ideas beyond payment for the price of their wares for their "positive externalities" (the social good they do).

In any case, says Professor Coase, economists should abandon their ambivalent attitude toward public policy in the market for ideas and the market for goods. Either they should favor increased government intervention in the market for ideas, or decreased government intervention in the market for goods. Or they could adopt an intermediate position, viewing government as neither so incompetent and base as it is assumed to be in the market for ideas nor so efficient and virtuous as it is assumed to be in the market for goods.

Professor William Baxter of the Stanford University Law School, who is both a lawyer and economist, contends that the press is less of a monopoly than it seems, although he does worry about local press monopolies. The percentage of American cities with two or more newspapers has fallen from about 60 percent in 1910 to less than 4 percent today. In the same period, the percentage of total daily newspaper circulation held by newspaper chains has risen from about 10 percent to 60 percent. By contrast, most major cities have three or four television stations; in the top 50 markets, the average number is about five TV stations—plus dozens of radio stations, AM and FM.

Yet Professor Baxter holds that such data are not relevant in determining the degree of diversity of news and opinion available to the public. The daily newspaper, he contends, faces plenty of competition from weekly news magazines, journals of opinion, and other periodicals, as well as from radio, television, books, advertisements, etc. Yet Professor Baxter is no great admirer of either newspapers or television. He accuses TV of "pablumizing" information and analysis for mass consumption, and implies that the press is little better. "Needless to say," he says, "I would opt for intervention if I could only be sure that I, or someone with my wisdom and insight, would be exerting the influence."

He concludes that government intervention to try to improve the press is "a frightening prospect unless the levers are in the hands of saints of great wisdom—and such men are in very short supply, particularly in government agencies."

Meanwhile, public-interest groups are pressing for greater competition and greater access for minority voices in both the print and electronic media. John Milton's *Areopagitica* has not lost its relevance, even where the problem is *private* rather than public monopoly. But there would appear to be no virtue in substituting government for private control, especially in the highly sensitive and important area of free speech.

The Failures of the Market

With all their virtues, markets have their failures in serving broad public interests. These may result from a lack of knowledge on the part of consumers, workers, or businessmen themselves; immobility of resources—workers in declining industries may, for instance, be unable to move to expanding industries; and side effects such as pollution or injury to personal health and well-being, which are not reflected in the normal pricing process and not corrected by the responses of the market. Recognition by economists of market failures goes back a long way—at least back to John Stuart Mill a century ago. In his *Essay on Liberty*[2] (1859), Mill said that "trade is a social act" but that the principle of individual liberty is not involved in the doctrine of "free trade," nor in most of the questions that arise over the limits of the doctrine.

For example, Mill asked, what amount of public control is

admissible for the prevention of fraud by adulteration? How far should sanitary precautions or arrangements to protect working people employed in dangerous occupations be enforced on employers? Such questions involve considerations of liberty only insofar as leaving people to themselves is always better, *ceteris paribus*, than controlling them. That they may, however, be legitimately controlled to prevent fraud or injury is, in principle, undeniable.

But there are questions relating to interference with trade which *are* essentially questions of liberty. The prohibition of the importation of opium into China and the restriction of the sale of poisons are, says Mill, typical of cases where the objective of the interference is to make it impossible or difficult to obtain a particular commodity. These interferences are objectionable as infringements on the liberty not of the producer or the seller, says Mill, but of the buyer.

Mill seeks to resolve this Nader-like issue. One of his examples, the sale of poisons, opens a new question—the proper limits of the police function, how far liberty can legitimately be invaded in order to prevent crime, accident, or disease.

It is one of the undisputed functions of government to take precautions against crime before it has been committed—as well as to detect and punish it after it has been committed.

But the preventive function of government, says Mill, is far more liable to be abused, with damage to individual freedom, than the punitive function. There is hardly anything a human being can do—flirt, loiter, read *Playboy*, drink beer—that could not be represented as tending toward some form or other of crime or delinquency.

Nevertheless, if a public authority, an off-duty policeman,

or a private person sees someone preparing to commit a crime, he is not required to wait until the crime has been committed, but may interfere to prevent it.

Does government have to wait until after a poison is used to ban its sale? The issue is tricky. Says Mill: "If poisons were never bought or used for any purpose except the commission of murders, it would be right to prohibit their manufacture and sale"—but they are not.

This problem continues to plague us. Should we ban the sale of handguns? Rifles?

What about products injurious to health but pleasant (at least in the judgment of some people) to use, such as cigarettes, whisky, marijuana, heroin, LSD?

Shall the public be protected from its own folly, and business prevented from making a profit? What about safety belts, air bags, helmets on motorcycle and moped riders, Laetrile?

Cases differ. And the conflicts they involve between individual freedom (or self-interest) and the public good (or bureaucratic power) must be resolved by some combination of pragmatism and idealism.

Pragmatism and Idealism: The Case of South Africa

Commercial interest may often be a better promoter of human rights and freedom than idealism—at least when idealism is in the service of a reactionary political creed.

In South Africa, for example, pressures against the government and its rigid doctrine of apartheid, the enforced system of racial separation and subordination, are coming from leaders of the business community—not just those of English descent but also from Afrikaners of Dutch, French, and German descent who have gained the commanding heights in finance, insurance, manufacturing, and other industries, and are losing their narrow, nationalistic perspective. It is the farmers, who want cheap black labor, and the lower-class white urban workers, who see blacks as competitors for jobs and wages, who provide the main political force behind apartheid.

This is why the governing Nationalist Party has been split into two wings, one called *verligte* (enlightened) and the other *verkrampte* (cramped or narrow-minded).

White liberalism in South Africa wears highly respectable garments. The principal backer of the anti-apartheid Progressive Party is Harry Oppenheimer, the multimillionaire chairman of the Anglo-American Corporation, which operates gold mines, diamond mines, and other enterprises.

One finds open or secret "Progs" throughout the business community—at the Johannesburg Stock Exchange, in banks, and at the mines. They preach a doctrine of enlightened self-interest. In addition to the need for a larger and better-trained work force (there is labor shortage among whites and unemployment among blacks), South African business leaders see vast opportunities for developing markets among the blacks. Business in South Africa is just making the discovery that Henry Ford made in the United States near the beginning of this century—that well-paid workers will not only produce more but will also be better customers for the goods produced.

The very low wages of black workers do not of course tell the whole story of their misery. For the migratory labor system requires millions of workers to leave their families in the "homelands," and they cannot send home enough money to prevent widespread hunger and malnutrition. Efforts of the blacks to organize and fight for their rights and better pay are frustrated by the government's picking off leaders by banning them from public activities, by brutal repression, spying, and massive imprisonment. Prison labor is extensively used on farms. Prison labor costs the farmer 15 cents a day per worker on weekdays and 10 cents a day on Saturdays.

Against present realities, modern South African businesses have visions of developing large new markets all over the African continent. They see Johannesburg becoming not only the workshop but the New York—the financial center— of Africa. But except for those countries directly surrounding South Africa and utterly dependent upon it for jobs, such as Botswana and Swaziland, that vision seems absurd to other black African nations, as long as the extreme repression and discrimination against blacks endure.

But South Africa remains in the thrall of its rigid ideology. The Nationalist leaders live in fear—fear of internal change and the rebellion that has now begun, fear of assault from the outside—by blacks backed by Communists—and this may not be a myth. Strangely enough, the Nationalist leaders, who are members of a party closely identified with the German Nazi party during the 1930's and World War II, now see a parallel between their cause and that of Israel.

The parallel seems ridiculous to some South African Jews, such as Helen Suzman, the courageous Progressive member of Parliament, who has often felt the lash of anti-Semitism from her political opponents. "I just love those aging photographs *Die Vaterland* uses—they make me look like a Jewish vulture eating small Christian children," said Mrs. Suzman.

153

The Nationalist government is not above using its power to curb or punish business supporters of progressive and anti-apartheid forces. On August 15, 1977, the *New York Times* correspondent in South Africa, John F. Burns, cabled:

> JOHANNESBURG—Relations between the South African Government and the country's largest business enterprise, Harry F. Oppenheimer's Anglo American Corporation of South Africa, often uneasy in recent years, have been strained anew by the Government's decision to block a $345 million deal under which Anglo American would have taken control of the state-owned manganese producer, South African Manganese Amcor Ltd.
>
> The decision has been widely interpreted in the business community as a political rebuff to Anglo American, the giant mining house, and to Mr. Oppenheimer personally. The 68-year-old executive has long been an opponent of the country's racial policies, and has spent millions of dollars of his own and his company's money to improve black education, housing and other interests. . . .
>
> In an editorial [*The Financial Mail*, the country's most influential business journal] said that the Government's move had been widely viewed in the financial community as "blatant discrimination" against the Oppenheimer concern. "If companies want to keep on the right side of the rules, it is now clear which side of the fence they must be on," it said.

Can business interests at last triumph peacefully over political ideology and fear in South Africa? Or must the resolution of the struggle between pragmatism and ideology be bloody and tragic?

Business Corruption, Political Extortion:
Lockheed and Bernhard

Business stands on a broad social base. Individual corporations and freedom of enterprise depend on the "consent" of the wider community. Whenever businessmen or politicians shock the community's sense of decency and fairness, free enterprise is threatened.

Among a host of instances of business-government corruption in recent years—and in many countries—one of the most shocking was the official statement by the Dutch government that Prince Bernhard, consort to the Queen, was open to "dishonorable requests and offers" from the Lockheed Aircraft Corporation. There was a clear implication in the official Dutch report—to which the Prince acceded in resigning from his position as inspector general of the armed forces and some three hundred other posts he held in Dutch military, business, and public organizations—that were it not for the threat to the monarchy, he would have been indicted on criminal charges.

Why did he do it? It made no political or economic sense. By the principle of Occam's razor, the simplest explanation seems to be the best: He just wanted the money. But, like so many similar acts of venality, his action failed the simplest test of conscience or prudence: "Would you do this if it were to become publicly known?" Disclosure—whether by the authorities or by an alert press—remains the most important social guarantor of moral behavior. But not all public or private business can be conducted in the open; hence the need for ingrained personal morality.

One of the slightly reassuring aspects of the Bernhard case is that the Dutch people—like the Americans after Watergate—have not lost their capacity to be shocked. Unfortunately, it may be that in some countries cynicism has already become so deep that the capacity to react to corruption is gone.

The Bernhard case drives home another point that has been stressed particularly by John J. McCloy, the distinguished lawyer whose report on Gulf Oil's illegal political contributions led to the removal of its chairman, Bob R. Dorsey: that government officials and legislators who solicit improper corporate payments are at least as culpable as the business executives who make them. Many businessmen feel that they have been more the victims of political extortions and shakedowns than voluntary bribers. That is not the universal case, but the initiative for corruption may have shifted to government as its weight in the economy has grown.

Cycles and Trends in Corruption

Back at the turn of the century, the journalist Lincoln Steffens saw the business-government balance the other way around: The "commercial sense of profit and loss," said Steffens, ruled American politics. The historian Thomas Beer wrote that Marcus Alonzo Hanna, the political boss who put William McKinley in the White House, was "technically not in politics at all. . . . He spent money on politicians."

That has become increasingly hard to do in the United States—although some politicians and businessmen may simply be waiting for the current storm to blow over.

There will surely continue to be cycles in business and political morality and immorality, as there have been in the past. The growing role of government in the economy and marketplace has doubtless intensified the problem. One can be sure that there will be future pressures, some of them extortionate, by government upon business—and future temptations for businessmen to bribe or at least pay off government officials and politicians. Even more than in the past, economics—especially business economics—cannot be divorced from politics.

Intelligent businessmen are coming to see that corrupt business-government relations are a menace to their companies and indeed to the private-enterprise system itself, both at home and abroad. Corruption exposes democratic societies to devastating attack by totalitarians of the left or the right.

But even when the Communist or Fascist threat seems insignificant, corruption deepens the distrust of a nation in its own political and economic institutions. It threatens the survival of a free and open society in which private enterprise and personal liberty can flourish.

If morality should atrophy within political, business, and labor organizations, all of our national and international problems would be seriously aggravated.

CHAPTER TEN

A Way of Reasoning

Most people react emotionally to economic issues—and to the very words in which they are expressed.

For instance, a *New York Times*-CBS public-opinion survey in the summer of 1977[1] discovered a strange contradiction: Most people were found to be deeply antagonistic to "welfare"—government welfare programs—but were strongly in favor of what welfare programs *do*.

The survey found that the word "welfare" raised a red flag before the public. But once the word was set aside, Americans from all walks of life showed compassion for the destitute and helpless. Of the 1,447 persons polled, 58 percent said that they disapproved of most government-sponsored welfare programs; and 54 percent agreed with the statement that "most people who receive money from welfare could get along without it if they tried."

But when they were asked a series of questions about the substance of welfare programs—questions in which the word "welfare" was omitted—people reacted very differently: 81 percent approved of the government's "providing financial assistance for children raised in low-income homes where one parent is missing." (This was a reference to what is the main component of welfare—Aid to Families with Dependent Children.) Similarly, 81 percent endorsed the government's "helping poor people buy food for their families at cheaper prices" (the essence of the food stamp program). And 82 percent said that they approved of using taxes to "pay for health care for poor people" (a reference to Medicaid). Remarkably enough, the response was much the same among the different types of people surveyed—rich and poor, liberal and conservative, Democrats and Republicans.

There are similar contradictions and confusions in public attitudes toward many other economic issues—government spending and taxation, the national debt, foreign aid, foreign trade, unemployment, job training, inflation, price controls, rent controls, fair trade laws, Federal aid for New York City —or other cities, health and safety laws, raising taxes on oil and gas, imposing price ceilings on natural gas, energy conservation, the minimum wage and its effect on unemployment, job discrimination, equal-opportunity laws, seniority rules, Social Security benefits, compulsory retirement rules, and much more.

People have very strong feelings about such issues but are often uncertain about where their own interests, or the broader social interests, really lie.

In dealing with controversial issues, economists try to separate professional analysis from their personal value judgments. This can never be done in a perfectly antiseptic way; even the choice of a problem involves some value judgment. Nor is there any way to keep alternative solutions absolutely value-free; the means chosen are affected by the ends desired.

Undoubtedly many economic problems are not solved systematically and "rationally" but by a stroke of insight or intuition. Yet a systematic effort to define, analyze, and choose among alternative solutions to problems can serve as a valuable check on blind prejudice masquerading as insight. Here are the stages in the "problem-solving" approach favored by most economists:[2]

1. *Define the problem or issue carefully—and assemble the relevant facts.*

Misconceived problems lead to faulty solutions. A classic example of this occurred during the Second World War when the United States Navy defined its problem in the North Atlantic as reducing the loss of merchant shipping to submarines. With the help of operations research, the Navy discovered that the German kill rate was inversely proportional to the size of convoys—the bigger the convoy, the lower the losses relative to the number of ships in a convoy. Hence, convoys were made bigger and bigger—and took longer and longer to assemble.

This *did* reduce shipping losses. But the main problem was how to win the war by moving matériel and manpower in the largest possible numbers, as fast as possible, to the battlefronts in Europe. While the huge convoys saved ship-

161

ping, they probably lengthened the war—and may have cost more lives as a result.

In our business and personal lives, it's essential to define our problems correctly. The top management of a supermarket chain was worried about profits and launched a cost-cutting drive. Interest came to focus on cutting the costs of bagging customers' orders. The decision was made to reduce the thickness of the paper and to provide different-sized bags to go with larger or smaller orders.

As a result, the supermarket chain's profits dropped further. Why? Customers were going to other stores where they still could count on getting bigger and stronger bags—which they could use for their trash and garbage. The chain's real problem was not the cost of its bags but the quality of its goods and the pull of its advertising.

Be careful that you don't try to solve the wrong problem.

2. *Identity the goals and objectives you hope to achieve.*

You alone know what you really want—and can determine your priorities or trade-offs among your different objectives. In his book *Working*, the great interviewer Studs Terkel has some marvelous examples of how people define their different goals. For instance, jazz musician Bud Freeman told Terkel:

> I get up about noon. I would only consider myself outside the norm because of the way other people live. . . . I wouldn't work for anybody. I'm working for me. Oddly enough, jazz is a music that came out of the black man's oppression, yet it allows for great freedom of expression, perhaps more than any other art form. The jazz man is expressing freedom in every note he plays. We can only please the audience doing what *we* do. We have to please ourselves first.

I know a good musician who worked for Lawrence Welk. The man must be terribly in need of money. It's regimented music. It doesn't swing. It doesn't create, it doesn't tell the story of life. It's just the kind of music that people who don't care for music would buy.

I've had people say to me: "You don't do this for a living, for Heaven's sake?" I was so shocked. I said, "What other way am I going to make a living? You want to send me a check?" [Laughs.] People can't understand that there are artists in the world as well as drones.[3]

Economics can't tell you to be like Bud Freeman. And it can't tell you to be like Lawrence Welk—or the "good musician" who played for Lawrence Welk. It can't tell you to give, or not give, the highest priority to making money or anything else. Admittedly, some critics of conventional economics do believe that it is biased toward materialistic objectives, but this is not an incorrigible fault. Strictly speaking, economics is not a system for prescribing goals for individuals or societies but a way of clarifying goals, discovering any conflicts among them, searching out means of reconciling or compromising different objectives, and of helping people to choose among the alternative routes toward achieving them.

Whatever your goals, you should at least be able to understand them without illusions—such as the "money illusion" that clouded the thinking of the officers of the New York Newspaper Guild in June 1976, when they issued the following bulletin:

Good news for all Guild members! The official May cost of living figures released last week added to that of the previous eleven months are reported to total

163

six and one-half percent. According to the terms of
our new agreement, Guild employees are to receive a
percentage equal to that amount above six percent.
Therefore, a raise is due each Guild member based
upon one half of one percent of your group top
minimum.

Thus, the good news was that money income was going up
half of one percent because real income had dropped over
six percent.

Money illusion may involve more than a confusion between money income and real income. It may also involve
confusing money income with what might be called "psychic
income"—the psychological rewards of work and creativity,
the knowledge that a job has been worth doing, the respect
of the public, and perhaps most important, self-respect.

Yet I must recognize that this may be a subjective view of
my own, which others would not accept or even respect.
When the muckraking newspaperman Lincoln Steffens ex-
posed how, and by whom, the corporation laws of New
Jersey had been written to enable trusts to be formed, and
wealth and power to be accumulated, he felt like a hero—
but wondered why the lawyer James B. Dill, who had written the laws, had helped Steffens expose them. "Why, Dr.
Innocent," Dill told him, "I was advertising my wares and
the business of my state. When you and the other reporters
and critics wrote as charges against us what financiers could
and did actually do in Jersey, when you listed, with examples, what the trust-makers were doing under our laws,
you were advertising our business—free. . . . While I gave
you the facts to roast us with, what you wrote as 'bad' struck
businessmen all over the United States as good, and they

poured in upon us to our profit to do business with us to their profit."[4]

What are your goals in life? Whatever they are, you should have the courage and intelligence to see them as clearly as Dill—or Lincoln Steffens.

3. *List the alternative means of attaining your goals.*

What are the constraints on your freedom of action? What resources do you have that will assist or limit your alternative routes? How much money do you have—or how much can you borrow? Who can help you, and how? What sacrifice will different solutions involve on your part? What risks are involved if you take one course or another? What will be the cost if you fail? What will be the payoff if you succeed?

Each alternative solution must be weighed and evaluated in the light of such questions—bringing to bear upon them as many relevant facts as you can muster.

4. *Identify the economic concepts needed to understand the problem you are working on, and analyze the alternatives in terms of those concepts.*

This is the critical test of how much economics you have learned. Economics is about *systems,* the interrelatedness of economic events. Awareness of the concept of *interdependence* should therefore always cause you to ask, "If I do this, what will X do? And if X does that, what will Y do?"

Walter Salant of the Brookings Institution gives an example of how as an economist he tends to think automatically about *interdependence,* even where the problem is not obviously an economic one. One morning Salant read that the police in Washington, D.C., had captured a large store of heroin. "The question that occurred to me," said Salant, "was whether the capture of a large amount of heroin might not raise the rate of robbery in Washington soon thereafter. I had in mind that if it really reduced the quantity of heroin available in the city, it would raise the price, perhaps considerably. This rise in prices would increase the pressure on users to get money; they would need more money, obviously, to buy the same quantity of heroin as they had been buying before. This might very well cause an increase in the rate of robbery, insofar as that is one of the means that addicts use to finance their purchase of drugs."[5] So the news of the seizure of a hoard of heroin made the economist Salant worry. Driving the price of heroin up might increase the "supply" of crime. What means might drive the price of heroin down? How about a methadone program? How about providing more heroin to addicts under a supervised medical program aimed at rehabilitation? What other means could be tried?

Whatever the problem you are working on, if you have begun to reason like an economist, you ought to be asking yourself: "What will happen then—and then—and then?" Solutions need to fit a whole interdependent system—not just one stage in a process.

Consider another economic concept—*marginalism*. The term sounds tricky, and indeed it is for most people, but it can simply be defined as "What's done is done," or "Let bygones be bygones." Suppose, for instance, that you are moving from a large house into a small apartment, and have to get rid of some of your furniture. You have a dining-room set that cost you $1,500 but have no room for it in the new apartment. How much should you sell it for? What if you are offered only $500? Should you take the "loss" of several hundred dollars—in relation to what you think it is really worth?

Probably the answer is "Sell it for whatever you can get—no matter what you paid for it." The original cost of the dining-room furniture is sunk. Why hold onto it, putting more money into storing it in a warehouse—unless you want to gamble on selling it at a higher price later. You've experienced the pleasure—the "psychic income"—of using it; now get some extra cash.

The same marginal concept applies to an airline (such as Southwest Airlines, as we saw) which is considering whether to run some extra flights to pick up additional revenue, even if the extra flights don't cover the fully allocated costs of equipment, computers, buildings, etc. Again, certain costs are already *sunk*—whether you run the extra flights or not, you can't get these costs back.

As long as the extra flights will return more than their out-of-pocket costs (such as additional gasoline, personnel costs, and landing fees) you will be better off—that is, have higher net earnings—than if you did not run the extra flights.

The marginal-cost, marginal-revenue principles should guide any business to the point where the *excess* of its total revenues over total costs (net profit) is greatest. It doesn't matter whether the problem is that of an airline, publishing house, individual lecturer, hot dog stand, railroad, movie house, or any other business activity, as the following simple example shows.

Here is how a typical business decision, involving the marginal concept, might be set up:

Problem: Shall we undertake Activity X?*
The Facts: Fully allocated costs of Activity X $4,500
            of which—

* Activity X could be a decision whether to run an extra airline flight, publish a new edition of a book, add a speaking engagement on a lecture

> Fixed or overhead costs are . .   2,500
> Out-of-pocket or marginal costs
> are   2,000
> Activity X should gross   3,100

Decision: Undertake Activity X. *It will add $1,100 to net profit.* The reason: X will add $3,100 to revenues and add only $2,000 to costs. (The fixed or overhead costs will be incurred whether X is done or not. Hence, fully allocated or average costs of $4,500 are *not* relevant to this business decision.) It is the out-of-pocket or marginal costs that count.

Many business decisions are mistakenly governed by the concept of fully allocated or average costs, instead of marginal costs, with a resulting loss in potential profits.

The right concept for dealing with a problem does not always come ready-made off the economist's shelf. Often one must struggle to fashion the concept that clarifies and solves a problem.

In 1959 I wrote a book called *The Research Revolution.* As it applied to individual companies, the book's main concept was:

> The principle and practice of making regular provision for the discovery and development of new ideas, new things, is taking increasing hold in American business. . . . More and more companies have come to regard expenditures for *research* not as a luxury but as a necessity to meet both domestic and foreign competition; many executives have come to refer to research

---

tour, sell hot dogs at a cheaper price after the seventh inning at a baseball game, offer half-price railroad or movie tickets for wives and children, or any other "marginal" activity.

as the lifeblood of successful business operation.... That a company has a strong and productive research program has come to be one sure way of judging management's competence and the company's growth prospects.[6]

I then named a group of companies that embodied the research concept and therefore promised stronger than average growth in sales and profits; the list included Haloid Xerox (later Xerox), Eastman Kodak, Polaroid, General Electric, General Telephone & Electronics, IBM, Minnesota Mining, RCA, National Cash Register, Schering, Pfizer, Texas Instruments, Thomas Ramo Wooldridge, Corning Glass, and several others that subsequently proved that the right concept pays off—big.

5. *Choose the alternative that appears to solve the problem best—and act on it.*

Of course, there's a good deal of hunch and "feel" about any important decision. But though hunch, feel, instinct, hope, fear, coolness, or other emotions inevitably play their parts in business and personal decisions, one ought to try to reach decisions on the best course to take by a process of reasoning that is systematic, thorough, and objective. That is what I have been trying to lay out here.

Finally, however, one must make up one's mind—and act on it decisively. Not to act is also a decision, and frequently the wrong one.

6. *Verify whether that alternative worked.*

If the plan didn't work, why not? Exactly what went wrong? There are crucial lessons to be learned for next time. Mistakes are part of the learning process—if you can survive them.

And if it *did* work out, the results should be carefully examined, too. You may have succeeded because of your original plan or in spite of it—and for unforeseen reasons. In Sir Francis Bacon's formulation of scientific method, verification is as important as observation, measurement, and explanation. Verification of a forecast or decision is the empirical test on which economic logic stands or falls.

Getting you into the habit of using the problem-solving approach is the main thing economics can do for you. The approach can be applied in any field and to virtually any kind of problem or issue. It's an approach that is liberating, not constricting; it invites you—forces you—to think outside the familiar frame of the problem. It prevents you from thinking off the top of your head and reacting compulsively and routinely. Making you weigh alternative solutions is what economics is all about.

CHAPTER ELEVEN

The Future of Economics

I took one draught of Life,
I'll tell you what I paid—
Precisely an existence—
The market price, they said.
      EMILY DICKINSON

The range of economics is astonishing: it reaches from the prosaic daily business of the marketplace and the factory to the great philosophical issues of human welfare, freedom, and equality—from the price of beans to the price of life.

Emily Dickinson's poem is doubtless meant to be ironical in making an analogy between market price and the payment of an "existence" for "one draught of life." But she was not the first to play upon the correspondence between the everyday business and the cosmic affairs of humanity.

Thomas Paine, in *The American Crisis* of 1776, wrote: "Heaven knows how to put a proper price upon its goods and it would be strange indeed, if so celestial an article as Freedom should not be highly rated."

And the most famous of our prayers asks the Lord to "give us this day our daily bread and forgive us our debts as we forgive our debtors."

There is no discontinuity in human affairs in any of its aspects, great or small. If economists have customarily taken as their subject matter the ordinary affairs of the market, the bank, or the government bureau, this does not mean that economics has nothing to do with the great issues of mankind. Quite the contrary. What Marshall called "the study of mankind in the ordinary business of life" has deep implications for all of human affairs, as people go about the work of creating values and organizing social systems. It was indeed the founding father of modern economics, Adam Smith, who sought to show the intricate connections between the daily business and the grand system of humankind. His formulation, rooted in the deist beliefs of the eighteenth century, now seems too simple for a world that has vastly increased in complexity.

The question is whether economics, in its current technical state, is capable of taking on so great a challenge as the exploration of the most profound and important issues affecting human society. Economists have built up an awe-inspiring body of theory, complete with fancy mathematics, that regrettably has only a tenuous relationship to the realities of politics, business, and the complex patterns of conflict and cooperation among individuals and nations.

As the gentle but iconoclastic economist Kenneth Boulding has put it: "I have been gradually coming under the conviction, disturbing for a professional theorist, that there is no such thing as economics—there is only social science applied to economic problems. Indeed, there may not even be such a thing as social science—there may only be general science applied to the problems of society."[1]

Yet those social problems, conventionally called economic, are among the most important that mankind has, and if they are not dealt with they can lead to still more awful problems —to the breakdown of societies and to wars. Somebody— economists and all of us—must try to deal with those difficulties rationally, and at the same time cope with the conflicting pressures of special interests, the confused value problems, the turbulent political contests, and the uncertain future that engulf economic decision making. It is no wonder, as we saw, that economists so frequently disagree. The differences among them, on both analytical and policy issues, often reflect the insecure state of their discipline, the poor state of their data, the narrowness of their conception of human behavior, the conflicts in their assumptions. And, as we sought to stress, many of their disputes come from their different values and, whether consciously or unconsciously, the economic and political interests they represent.

Gunnar Myrdal, a Swedish Nobel Prize winner for his work on a range of problems as diverse as race relations in the United States and poverty and economic development in Asia and Africa, is convinced that "problems in the social sciences—not only the practical ones about what ought to be done, but also the theoretical problems of ascertaining the facts and the relations among facts—cannot be rationally posited except in terms of definite, concretized, and explicit value premises." Curiously enough, the libertarian economist and philosopher Friedrich von Hayek, who shared the Nobel

Prize with Myrdal, regards Myrdal's kind of socialist economics as "the road to serfdom"—yet agrees with Myrdal that economics rests on a base of social and moral values, which differ from economist to economist, and from person to person or society to society. Hayek sees no hope of establishing a "value-free" or "scientific" economics along the lines of physics or chemistry; he criticizes economists who try to model their discipline on the natural sciences as "scientistic," that is, falsely scientific.

One Science or Many?

Regarding economics in its present state of disarray, one still may ask, as St. Thomas Aquinas asked about philosophy in his *Summa Theologica:* "Is this one science or many?"

The answer would seem to be, certainly at the level of national and global policy, that economics is not only many sciences but also something more—a branch of statecraft, of political philosophy, in which analytical method and technique cannot substitute for intuition and judgment. Keynes, probably the greatest economist of this century, once described the singular difficulties of economics in this way:

"Professor Planck, of Berlin, the famous originator of the quantum theory, once remarked to me that in early life he had thought of studying economics, but had found it too difficult! Professor Planck could easily master the whole corpus of mathematical economics in a few days. He did not mean that! But the amalgam of logic and intuition and the wide knowledge of facts, most of which are not precise, which is required for economic interpretation in its highest form is, quite truly, overwhelmingly difficult for those whose gift mainly consists in the power to imagine and pursue to their furthest points the implications and prior conditions of comparatively simple facts which are known with a high degree of precision."[2]

In brief, the job of the economist calls for a genius, and genius is as rare in economics as in music, literature, the natural sciences, or any other field—maybe rarer. But economics has had some geniuses, such as Smith, Malthus, and Marx. The great problems they addressed—the growth in the wealth of nations and human freedom; the growth of population, the limits of resources, and the persistence of poverty; the class structure and the power of capital; the new technology and the dehumanization of work; equity and efficiency; economic evolution and revolution— remain with us, still unsolved.

The Unsolved Riddles

The problems change their appearance somewhat from generation to generation, from age to age, but they are the same old problems of human development and threats to human survival. And we grow weary of the old problems and the intellectualizing about them that goes on forever. We are tempted to say, like Sabina in Thornton Wilder's play *The Skin of Our Teeth:* "I hate this play and every word of it. As for me, I don't understand a single word of it, anyway—all about the troubles the human race has gone through, there's a subject for you."

Many people have had the same reaction to *The Limits*

to Growth, the report for the Club of Rome's Project on the Predicament of Mankind that provoked such widespread and angry debate a few years ago. We have already got comfortable with the "limits to growth" doomsaying; and that kind of complacent reaction, as Thornton Wilder seemed to be saying through his character Sabina, appears to be one of the ways that the Antrobus (All Mankind) family preserves its sanity and survives.

But it's not the only way. George Antrobus' ingenuity in solving problems, as well as his stubborn determination to accommodate himself to any misery, kept him going through the Ice Age. Pure luck saved him and the rest of his family and their animals during the Great Flood. Even worse dangers assailed him as a result of his brother's destructive spirit—from Cain through Caligula to Tojo and Hitler; they were defeated by a funny mixture of morality and ferocity and cleverness.

But has the greatest threat of all to humanity now come in a most seductive and seemingly innocent form—mankind's sincere desire to be rich—and its command of technology to achieve that end?

Such is the thesis of the Club of Rome report.[3] Its authors —Donella Meadows, Dennis Meadows, and a team of scientists from the Massachusetts Institute of Technology—used a computerized model, derived from a still more elaborate model created by Professor Jay W. Forrester, to predict that "if the present growth trends in world population, industrialization, pollution, food production, and resource depletion continue unchanged, the limits to growth on this planet will be reached sometime within the next one hundred years." The most probable result of this, they predicted, would be "a rather sudden and uncontrollable decline in both population and industrial capacity."

This tragedy, they contended, would result from the malignant feedbacks produced by an industrial system designed to provide humanity with ever-increasing benefits. More specifically, the model postulates that the creation of capital—real capital in the form of factories, mines, generators, nuclear reactors, trucks, trains, planes, etc.—causes economic growth; greater wealth and expanding technology cause population to go on mounting, as death rates fall faster than birth rates. But a greater population, producing more and more, as the poor strive to catch up with the rich and the rich try to get richer and richer, pollutes the earth and exhausts its resources.

For a little while longer, the model indicates, the world economic system can go on agglomerating capital and people in urban sprawl, but finally a limit will be reached. Why? Because population, capital, and pollution all grow at exponential rates (not just population, as Malthus said) like money at compound interest; but the earth and its resources are finite, says the MIT team, and they cannot be stretched indefinitely by new technology. Entropy, the dissipation of earthly resources and energy through the industrial process, adds Professor Nicholas Georgescu-Roegen,[4] cannot be arrested by some technological miracle.

But when will the exhaustion of earthly resources come? When will the human tragedy occur?

No scientific answer is yet possible; the greater part of the empirical job is still to be done, and may never be done. The complexity of modeling a reliable economic-social-physical-biological - scientific - technological - industrial - demographic

177

world system for forecasting purposes goes far beyond anything the MIT team has done. Further, human ingenuity may modify economic and social systems, check pollution, develop new energy sources, reduce or reverse population growth, go beyond earthly limits.

So questions must be raised about the imminence of the disaster that the MIT team foresees and about the model and empirical data on which their predictions are based.

Does this mean that the Club of Rome report is all wrong? Not necessarily. Even an ever-expanding pool of resources can be poisoned. And even if total disaster should not lurk around the corner, life in an ever-expanding industrial system can become wretchedly crowded, dirty, mean, and dangerous. And the worst danger may be in Antrobus' ability to accommodate himself to almost anything, as he has done before. "The real horror, Kuprin," said Dostoevsky, "is that there is no horror."

The argument for continuing economic growth for a while longer is very strong. Hundreds of millions of people throughout the world live in desperate poverty, and their problems cannot be solved by redistribution of existing world income. Furthermore, world population is certain to go on growing for many years to come. The United Nations projects world population, which was three billion in 1960 and has grown to more than four billion now, to reach seven billion by the end of the century. Even if that rate of population increase can be slowed, economic growth will be essential to prevent worsening misery, starvation, chaos, and war. In a world of no economic growth, one nation's—or one person's—advance would necessarily mean another's decline, and conflicts would proliferate and intensify. Are we yet ready to declare that we have attained "Pareto optimality"?

A Revolution of the Mind

Yet it is a fact that our industrial society is getting danger-ously crowded, complex, and putrid. We urgently need a change in social values—a shift in our goals from increasing the quantity of production to improving the quality of life. Almost the whole of our society and its institutions, business and governmental, is geared to growth of the old kind; the shift can occur only if we have what has correctly been called "a Copernican Revolution of the mind." We have scarcely begun to think through what that would mean in terms of the use of resources, conservation, employment, education, income distribution, the location as well as the size of population, social and economic incentives and dis-incentives, structural changes in the economy and industry —if changing from quantity to quality were to become our dominant social purpose.

The task is obviously one that goes far beyond the limits of existing economics, as the most sensitive economists well realize. After a long spell of quiet and even smugness about the state of their science, economists are asking themselves the most fundamental questions about what they should be doing and how. Their answers may turn out to be important for solving some of the most perplexing and stubborn prob-lems afflicting humanity. They may ultimately have a great deal to do with how men and nations can be helped to be-have more decently and sensibly, with less harm to one another.

Perhaps some danger exists that economics—a limited field but one with some significant achievements behind it —will drown prematurely in a sea of related disciplines and philosophical speculations before it has adequately solved

179

some of its own traditional problems, such as how simultaneously to achieve full employment and price stability, and how to put together a stable, essentially free, and expanding world economy.

Yet it seems to me that efforts to solve even those traditional economic problems cannot be hampered, but only advanced, by a deeper understanding of many matters that lie beyond the boundaries of conventional economics.

APPENDIX
Statistical Concepts

Some simple statistical or mathematical concepts will help you to understand economic articles—and protect you from misrepresentation.

1. Averages and Distributions Around the Average

There are different ways to measure the central tendency of any series of numbers, such as people's incomes.

The most commonly used is the *mean* (or "average"), which is computed by dividing the sum of the incomes by the total number of individual people represented in the series.

The *median* is a point on a scale of measurement above which are half the cases and below which are the other half (in the

cases of incomes, it is the point that separates the 50 percent
with higher incomes from the 50 percent with lower incomes).

The *mode* is the value (or income) which occurs with the
greatest frequency.

Thus if we have ten persons with the following annual incomes:

Anne	$ 5,000
Bill	6,000
Charley	8,000
Dave	10,000
Eleanor	10,000
Frank	11,000
Gertrude	14,000
Harry	20,000
Ida	30,000
Michael	100,000
	Total $214,000

the *mean* (average) income is $21,400 ($214,000 divided by 10);
the *median* is $10,500 (above which are F, G, H, I, and M, and
below which are A, B, C, D, and E); and the *mode* is $10,000
(the largest single class, which contains D and E).

In the above series, Michael's high income makes the *mean* a
somewhat misleading measure of central tendency. The *median*
or *mode* may better convey the typical income level of the group
as a whole. But ordinarily the *mean* is the most useful measure
of central tendency or "average."

In making international comparisons, it is important to notice
the difference between total and average (or per capita) Gross
National Product. The People's Republic of China, for example,
in 1970 had a GNP of $121.8 billion and Sweden had a GNP of
$32.5 billion. But China was poor and Sweden rich; for China's
population was 836 million, and its per capita GNP was $160 a
year, while Sweden's population was a little over 8 million, and
its per capita GNP was $4,040—25 times as much as China's.

Appendix: Statistical Concepts

An average tells you nothing about the distribution around an average. An old statistical joke goes: "I lay with my head in the refrigerator and my feet in the stove, and on the average I was comfortable." The United States has a high average GNP but a lot of poor people, and Mexico a relatively low average GNP but a lot of rich people—while East (Communist) Germany has a fairly high per capita GNP and very few rich people. The per capita GNP in 1970 of the United States was $4,760; Mexico, $670; and East Germany, $2,490—but here is how income was distributed among their populations:

SIZE DISTRIBUTION OF INCOME, U.S., MEXICO, AND E. GERMANY

Percent of Population	PERCENT OF NATIONAL INCOME		
	United States	Mexico	East Germany
0–10	1.4	2.0	4.0
10–20	3.4	2.2	6.4
20–30	4.6	2.7	7.5
30–40	5.9	3.3	8.4
40–50	7.1	4.3	9.3
50–60	8.6	5.4	10.3
60–70	10.4	7.2	11.1
70–80	12.8	9.7	12.3
80–90	16.7	14.4	13.8
90–100	29.1	48.8	16.9
	100.0	100.0	100.0

Thus, in the United States, the poorest 10 percent of the population received only 1.4 percent of the national income, while in Mexico the lowest 10 percent received 2 percent of the national income, and in East Germany the bottom 10 percent got 4 percent of that income. In the United States, the top 10 percent of the population got 29.1 percent of the national income, compared with 48.8 percent and 16.9 percent of national income going to the top 10 percent of the population in Mexico and East Germany, respectively. Thus income distribution appears to be most *unequal* in poor capitalist countries like Mexico, where 10 percent of the population gets almost half the income.

2. Real Versus Nominal GNP

Gross National Product represents an attempt to measure the dollar value of final goods currently produced. It is called "gross" because it includes charges for replacing depreciating (wearing-out) assets. And it measures final products, rather than intermediate products, to avoid double counting.

Nominal GNP measures total current output in *current dollars*—that is, in terms of what they are currently worth in the marketplace, given present prices.

Real GNP represents expenditures on total current output as measured by dollars worth what they were in some earlier (base) year, such as 1972, given what prices then were.

The following table shows the differences between nominal and real GNP from 1972 through the second quarter of 1977:

Year	(1) Nominal GNP (in current dollars) (billions)	(2) Price Index (called the "implicit price deflator") with 1972 = 100 (percentage)	(3) Real GNP (column 1 divided by column 2 times 100)—corrected for inflation (billions)
1972	$1,171.6	100.00	$1,171.1
1973	1,306.6	105.80	1,235.0
1974	1,412.9	116.02	1,217.8
1975	1,528.8	127.18	1,202.1
1976	1,706.5	133.88	1,274.7
1977	1,890.4	141.32	1,337.6

Appendix: Statistical Concepts

Notice that nominal GNP in the second quarter of 1977 was over 40 percent higher than real GNP, relative to nominal (and real) GNP in 1972. Inflation accounted for the difference.

3. Amounts Versus Rates

We need to distinguish between the *amounts* of GNP (whether nominal or real) and the *rates* of growth of GNP, to measure how output is changing. The following table states the rates of GNP growth (or shrinkage) since 1972 in both nominal and real terms, together with the rates of inflation, as measured by the implicit price deflator.

Annual Rates of Change, GNP and Prices
(percentages)

Year	Nominal GNP	Real GNP	Price Deflator
1972	10.1	5.7	4.1
1973	11.6	5.5	5.8
1974	8.1	−1.4	9.7
1975	8.2	−1.3	9.6
1976	11.6	6.0	5.3
1977	10.8	4.9	5.6

Notice that the recession of 1974–75 does not show up in the nominal GNP column, since, in current dollars, GNP advanced by 8.1 percent and 8.2 percent in those two years. But, when corrected for inflation (9.7 percent and 9.6 percent for 1974 and 1975 respectively), real GNP registered the recession by declining by 1.4 percent in 1974 and by 1.3 percent in 1975. As measured by the implicit price deflator, inflation in those two years was just short of double-digit rates. But the wholesale and consumer price indexes recorded double-digit rates in 1974 and, in the case of wholesale prices, in 1973 as well, as the following table shows:

Appendix: Statistical Concepts

Rates of Increase in Price Indexes
(percentages)

Year	Wholesale Prices	Consumer Prices
1972	6.3	3.4
1973	15.4	8.8
1974	20.9	12.2
1975	4.2	7.0
1976	4.7	4.8
1977	6.2	6.6

4. Index Numbers

In the examples above, we have been using index numbers to measure relative price changes over time. Other index numbers can be constructed and calculated for changes in production, employment, sales, or any other data. The index number simply measures percentage changes from a base period. There are, however, many complexities in calculating index numbers, depending on which components are chosen to be included, how the components are weighted, whether their composition changes from year to year, what base period is chosen, etc. If an unusually good or an unusually bad year is chosen as the base, this may distort future comparisons.

Though index numbers are usually used for comparing changes in data over time, they can also be used to make comparisons between places or other categories, such as changes in living costs between different cities or states, changes in production in different countries, or the relative efficiency of different types of machinery.

5. Ratios

Ratios express the relationship of one numerical value to another. The ratio of black to white unemployment usually is a ratio of

186

2:1. If a bottle of milk costs 60¢ and a bus ride 30¢ their ratio is also 2:1.

The price-earnings (p/e) ratio of a company's stock is the earnings per share of the company divided into its current market price. Thus, if a company's current rate of annual earnings is $231 million, and it has 55 million shares outstanding, its earnings per share equal $4.20. And if that company's stock is selling for $56 per share, its price-earnings ratio is 13.3:

$$\frac{\text{Price per share}}{\text{Earnings per share}} = \frac{\$56}{\$4.20} = 13.3$$

6. Tables

We have already used several examples of tables; their chief purpose is to facilitate comparisons that would otherwise be hard to get straight in our heads. Take the following comparisons of industrial production in the United States, Canada, and Japan in recent years:

Industrial Production
(1967 = 100)

Year	United States	Canada	Japan
1974	129.3	146.6	187.6
1975	117.8	139.7	167.4
1976	129.8	146.3	190.0

The table above helps the reader to play whatever games he wants with the data—and perhaps to regard them differently from the author.

7. Graphs and Charts

Tables can readily be turned into graphs or charts to dramatize comparisons. The above data on industrial production can, for instance, be represented by the following graph:

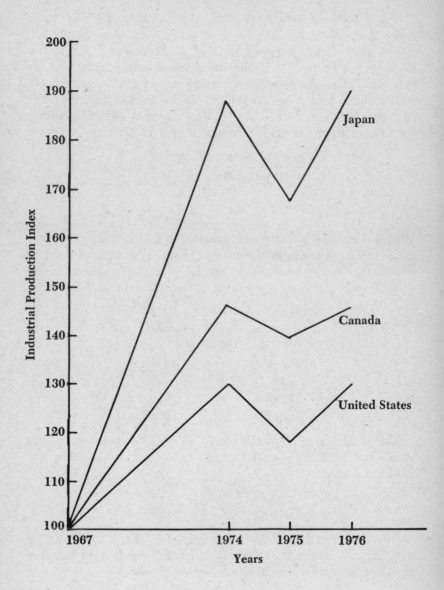

or by this bar chart:

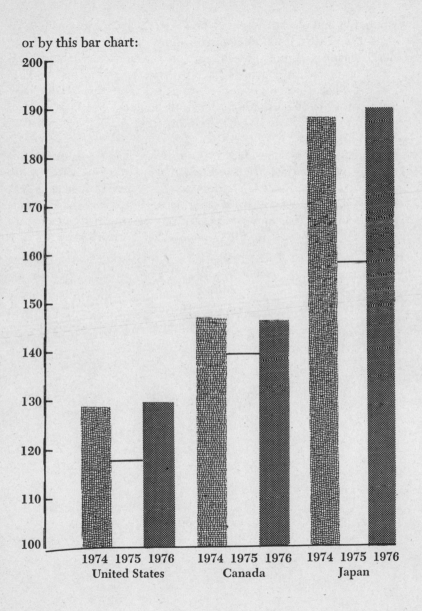

Appendix: Statistical Concepts

Graphs and charts can easily be drawn in such a way as to mislead the reader; small changes in numbers can be blown up, or large changes shrunk, by changes in the vertical or horizontal scale of a chart, by not using a zero base, by the misuse of bars or drawings, etc. Statistics *don't* speak for themselves; like words, they can be used honestly or dishonestly. See Darrell Huff and Irving Geis, *How to Lie with Statistics* (W. W. Norton & Co., New York, 1954).

Statistical data themselves need to be examined critically—not just the way the data are presented. Oskar Morgenstern's *On the Accuracy of Economic Observations* (Princeton University Press, Princeton, N.J., 1970) is a masterpiece of statistical criticism— and a warning to economists against relying on grossly inaccurate data (including those on the Gross National Product).

Notes

Chapter One

1. *The New Yorker*, "Talk of the Town," June 27, 1977.
2. Alfred Marshall, *Principles of Economics* (1st ed.) (The Macmillan Co., New York, 1948).
3. Harvey Leibenstein, *Beyond Economic Man* (Harvard University Press, Cambridge, Mass., 1976).
4. George Katona, "Economics as a Behavioral Science," in *Frontiers in Social Thought, Essays in Honor of Kenneth E. Boulding*, Martin Pfaff, ed. (North-Holland Publishing Company, New York, 1976).

Chapter Two

1. For a boiled-down version of Adam Smith's great work, see *Selections from the Wealth of Nations*, George Stigler, ed. (Appleton-Century-Crofts, c1957). For further reading in the history of economic thought, see Robert L. Heilbroner, *The Worldly Philoso-*

Notes

phers, and Joseph A. Schumpeter, *History of Economic Analysis*, both cited in "Suggestions for Further Reading," below. The reader who has time and interest will find Smith's classic *Wealth of Nations* both readable and fascinating in its details.

2. There are many editions of *The Communist Manifesto;* one is cited in the suggested readings below. The work hits like a sledge hammer. By comparison, Marx's *Das Kapital* (*Capital*) is tough going.
3. For a sympathetic interpretation of Marx, see Michael Harrington, *Socialism* (Saturday Review Press, New York, 1972).
4. E. F. Schumacher, *Small Is Beautiful* (Harper & Row, New York, 1973).
5. Donella H. Meadows, *et al.*, *The Limits to Growth* (Universe Books, Washington, D.C., c1972).
6. Kenneth J. Arrow, *Information and Economic Behavior* (Federation of Swedish Industries, Stockholm, 1973).

Chapter Three

1. Paul A. Samuelson, *Foundations of Economic Analysis* (Harvard University Press, Cambridge, Mass., 1948).
2. Walter Salant, "Writing and Reading in Economics," *The Journal of Political Economy*, Vol. 77, No. 4, Part 1 (July/August, 1969).
3. George Orwell, "Politics and the English Language," in G. Orwell, *Inside the Whale and Other Essays* (Penguin Books, London, 1965).
4. Fred M. Westfield, "Innovation and Monopoly Regulation," in William M. Capron, ed., *Technological Change in Regulated Industries* (The Brookings Institution, Washington, D.C., 1971), pp. 15–16. I confess that I had a hand in editing Professor Westfield's chapter when I was a Senior Fellow at Brookings.
5. Moses Abramovitz and Paul A. David, "Reinterpreting Economic Growth: Parables and Realities," *The American Economic Review*, Papers and Proceedings of the [1972] Eighty-fifth Annual Meeting of the American Economic Association, May 1973, pp. 433–434.

In offering the above two selections of Economese for translation, I sought to be fair to the economics profession. The reader may be interested in examining for his pleasure a couple of other passages that I seriously considered using from the same Annual Proceedings volume from which the Abramovitz-David (A-D) article was taken:

Notes

The problem of optimal search from a literally unknown distribution is intractable without some restrictions on the admissible distributions. Even those who are willing to embrace a Bayesian approach can handle only that case which specifies a subset of all possible probability distributions and assigns a prior probability to each member of the subset. In this case the optimal rule specifies a maximum acceptable price which changes with the accumulation of new evidence from trial to trial as a result of the revisions of the prior distributions. With complete ignorance about the nature of the probability distributions, save for assuming that all have a finite range, it does not seem fruitful to assign equal prior probabilities to each admissible distribution. Therefore, it is worth exploring a different approach to the problem when there is complete ignorance.
[L. G. Telser, "Searching for the Lowest Price," A.E.A. 1972 Proceedings, op. cit., p. 44.]

Next:

How does a reduction in the number of revision periods until the terminal date influence the optimum ratio of risky assets in the portfolio? Analysis considered here of this aspect of the decision problem integrates the characteristics of the intertemporal investment opportunity set. Postulate the following investment scenario: It is a two-parameter mean-variance world whereby the distributions of terminal wealth are lognormally distributed and there is one risky asset (the market portfolio) and one riskless asset. Further, the investor is locked in due to high transaction costs with regard to the optimal risky asset ratio. [James L. Bicksler, Amir Barnea, and Jair Babad, "Portfolio Choice, the Horizon Problem and the Investment Opportunity Set," A.E.A. 1972 Proceedings, op. cit., p. 141.] [Author's note: From the average economist's point of view, this is indeed a mean-variance world, full of lousy, mean-variance people.]

Chapter Six

1. See Leonard Silk and M. Louise Curley, A Primer on Business Forecasting (Random House, New York, 1970).

Notes

Chapter Eight

1. For an enlightening discussion of empirical fact versus logic, see Taylor Branch, "New Frontiers in American Philosophy," *The New York Times Magazine,* August 14, 1977.
2. Andrew Dickson White, *Fiat Money Inflation in France* (The Caxton Printers, Ltd., Caldwell, Idaho, 1974, originally published in 1876).
3. Leonard Silk, *Nixonomics* (Praeger, New York, 1972), p. 184.

Chapter Nine

1. Leonard Silk, "Free Press: A Topic for Economists," *The New York Times,* Dec. 23, 1973.
2. John Stuart Mill's *Essays on Liberty* (1859) is available in many editions, most conveniently in Everyman's Library, New York, c1914.

Chapter Ten

1. *The New York Times,* August 3, 1977, p. 1.
2. See *A Framework for Teaching Economics: Basic Concepts* (Joint Council on Economic Education, New York, 1977) for a similar formulation of the process of economic reasoning, as well as Leonard Silk, *Contemporary Economics: Principles and Issues* (McGraw-Hill Book Company, New York, 1970, 1975), especially pp. 10–14 in the 1975 edition.
3. Studs Terkel, *Working* (Avon Books, New York, 1972), pp. 596–597.
4. Lincoln Steffens, *The Autobiography of Lincoln Steffens* (Harcourt, Brace and Company, New York, 1931), p. 195.
5. Walter Salant, "Writing and Reading in Economics," *op. cit.*
6. Leonard Silk, *The Research Revolution* (McGraw-Hill Book Company, New York, 1960), pp. 176–177.

Chapter Eleven

1. Kenneth E. Boulding, *A Reconstruction of Economics* (Wiley, New York, 1950), p. vii.

Notes

2. J. M. Keynes, *Essays in Biography* (Macmillan, Cambridge, England, 1972, first edition 1933), p. 186.
3. Donella H. Meadows, *et al., The Limits to Growth, op. cit.*
4. Nicholas Georgescu-Roegen, "The Entropy Law and the Economic Problem," Distinguished Lecture Series No. 1, December 3, 1970, Department of Economics and Office for International Programs, The University of Alabama.

Suggestions for Further Reading

Economics as a Discipline

Kenneth E. Boulding, *Economics as a Science*. McGraw-Hill, New York, 1970.
Joseph A. Schumpeter, *History of Economic Analysis*. Oxford University Press, New York, 1954.

Biographies of Economists

Robert L. Heilbroner, *The Worldly Philosophers: The Lives, Times, and Ideas of the Great Economic Thinkers*. Simon and Schuster, New York, 1961.
Paul H. Douglas, *In the Fullness of Time*. Harcourt Brace Jovanovich, New York, 1972.

Suggestions for Further Reading

John Maynard Keynes, *Essays in Biography*. Macmillan, St. Martin's Press, London and New York, 1972.

Leonard Silk, *The Economists*. Basic Books, New York, 1976.

Economic History

Harvey C. Bunke, *A Primer on American Economic History*. Random House, New York, 1969.

Charles P. Kindleberger, *The World in Depression, 1929–1939*. University of California Press, Berkeley, 1973.

R. H. Tawney, *Religion and the Rise of Capitalism*. New American Library, New York, 1954.

Studs Terkel, *Hard Times, An Oral History of the Great Depression*. Avon Books, New York, 1971.

Economic Systems

Gregory Grossman, *Economic Systems*. Prentice-Hall, Englewood Cliffs, N.J., 1973.

Michael Harrington, *Socialism*. Saturday Review Press, New York, 1972.

Karl Marx and Friedrich Engels, *The Communist Manifesto*, with selections from *The Eighteenth Brumaire of Louis Bonaparte* and *Capital*. Edited by Samuel H. Beer. Appleton-Century-Crofts, Boston, written in 1848, published 1955.

Richard Romano and Melvin Leiman, *Views on Capitalism*. Glencoe Press, Glencoe, Ill., 1970.

Joseph A. Schumpeter, *Capitalism, Socialism, and Democracy*. Harper & Row, New York, 1962.

Economic Goals

Milton Friedman, *Capitalism and Freedom*. University of Chicago Press, Chicago, 1972.

Suggestions for Further Reading

John Kenneth Galbraith, *Economics and the Public Purpose*. Houghton Mifflin, Boston, 1973.

Arthur M. Okun, *Equality and Efficiency*. The Brookings Institution, Washington, D.C., 1975.

Henry Owen and Charles L. Schultze, *Setting National Priorities: The Next Ten Years*. The Brookings Institution, Washington, D.C., 1976.

E. F. Schumacher, *Small Is Beautiful: Economics as if People Mattered*. Harper & Row, New York, 1973.

Economic Growth

Donella H. Meadows *et al.*, *The Limits to Growth*. Universe Books, Washington, D.C., 1972.

E. J. Mishan, *The Economic Growth Debate: An Assessment*. George Allen & Unwin, London and Reading, Mass., 1977.

Peter Passell and Leonard Ross, *Affluence and Its Enemies*. Viking Press, New York, 1973.

W. W. Rostow, *The Stages of Economic Growth: A Non-Communist Manifesto*. Cambridge University Press, Cambridge, England, 1960.

Microeconomics

Robert Dorfman, *Prices and Markets*. Prentice-Hall, Englewood Cliffs, N.J., 1972.

Joseph McKenna, *The Logic of Price*. Dryden Press, New York, 1973.

Macroeconomics

Robert L. Heilbroner, *Understanding Macroeconomics*. Prentice-Hall, Englewood Cliffs, N.J., 1972.

Charles L. Schultze, *National Income Analysis*. Prentice-Hall, Englewood Cliffs, N.J., 1972.

Money

Peter L. Bernstein, *A Primer on Money, Banking, and Gold*. Random House, New York, 1968.

Suggestions for Further Reading

James S. Duesenberry, *Money and Credit: Impact and Control.* Prentice-Hall, Englewood Cliffs, N.J., 1972.

Lawrence S. Ritter and William L. Silber, *Money: A Guide to the 1970's.* Basic Books, New York, 1970.

Economic Reasoning

Abba P. Lerner, *Everybody's Business: A Re-examination of Current Assumptions in Economics and Public Policy.* Harper & Row, New York, 1961.

E. J. Mishan, *Popular Economic Fallacies.* Praeger Publishers, New York, 1973.

Marshall A. Robinson *et al., An Introduction to Economic Reasoning.* Doubleday, New York, 1967.

Leonard Silk and M. Louise Curley, *A Primer on Business Forecasting.* Random House, New York, 1970.

Statistical Methods

John E. Freund and Frank J. Williams, *Modern Business Statistics.* Prentice-Hall, Englewood Cliffs, N.J., 1958.

Marty J. Schmidt, *Understanding and Using Statistics: Basic Concepts,* D. C. Heath and Company, Lexington, Mass., 1975.

W. Allen Wallis and Harry V. Roberts, *Statistics: A New Approach.* The Free Press, Glencoe, Ill., 1958.

Statistical Criticism

Darrell Huff and Irving Geis, *How to Lie with Statistics.* W. W. Norton, New York, 1954.

Oskar Morgenstern, *On the Accuracy of Economic Observations.* Princeton University Press, Princeton, N.J., 1963.

Sources of Economic Data

The Budget of the United States. Annually. Executive Office of the President, Office of Management and Budget, Government Printing Office (GPO).

Suggestions for Further Reading

Census of Manufactures. U.S. Department of Commerce, GPO.

Economic Indicators. Monthly. Prepared for the Joint Economic Committee of Congress by the Council of Economic Advisers, GPO.

Economic Report of the President. Annually. GPO.

Federal Reserve Bulletin. Monthly. Board of Governors of the Federal Reserve System, Washington, D.C. 20551.

Monthly Labor Review. Monthly. U.S. Department of Labor, GPO.

Statistical Abstract of the United States. Annually. U.S. Department of Commerce, Bureau of the Census, GPO.

Survey of Current Business. Monthly. U.S. Department of Commerce, GPO.

Acknowledgments

This book began as an article, "Economics for the Perplexed," which I wrote for *The New York Times Magazine* of March 2, 1975. I appreciate the publisher's permission to draw upon this and other articles and columns which I have written for *The New York Times* in recent years.

I am also grateful to the Joint Council on Economic Education, on whose board of trustees I have served for the past two decades, for its pioneering work in improving the quality and increasing the quantity of economic instruction in high schools, colleges, universities and even in the primary schools. The report *A Framework for Teaching Economics: Basic Concepts* by the Joint Council's Master Curriculum committee—W. Lee Hansen, chairman, G. L. Bach, James D. Calderwood, and Phillip Saunders—was particularly helpful to me in writing this book.

Acknowledgments

I am deeply indebted for invaluable research assistance to my son, Andrew Silk, a recent fellow of the Thomas J. Watson Foundation, and to Kristin SerVaas, a student at the Harvard Graduate School of Business.

I wish to thank my editor, Michael Korda, for many good suggestions and much good advice. I also owe thanks to my *Times* colleague Israel Shenker for his piece on Leibel Bistritzky, published anonymously in *The New Yorker* of June 27, 1977—a piece that brilliantly captured the idea that economics need not be for bread or money alone. I am in the debt of Professor Harvey Leibenstein of Harvard University for his book *Beyond Economic Man*, in which he developed the same idea in profound theoretical terms. My debts to other economists, living and dead, are too numerous for specific acknowledgment.

L.S.

Index

205

Index

Balance of payments (*cont.*)
  dollar devaluation and, 111
  European recovery and, 105–06
  unemployment and, 121
Balance-of-payments deficit, 106–109
Baxter, William, 148
Bee colony, society compared with, 28–29
Beer, Thomas, 156
Berlinguer, Enrico, 137
Bernhard, Prince (Netherlands), 155
Bistritzky, Leibel, 17
Boom-depression cycle, 16
Borrowing, profits and, 60
Boulding, Kenneth, 31, 172–73
Boulware, Lemuel, 61
Bourgeoisie, capitalism and, 16
Braniff Airlines, 140–42
Bretton Woods Agreement, 107–108, 113
Bronowski, J., 15
Brookings Institution, 49, 165
Browne, Malcolm, 77
"Buddhist" economy, 40
Burns, Arthur F., 131–32
Burns, John F., 154
Business, in economic theory, 20
Business corruption, 155–57
Business cycle, 16, 101
Business decisions, economic concepts in, 168
Businessmen
  borrowing by, 60
  instincts of, 22–23

Calumet Mutual Insurance Company, 143

Cambodia, economy of, 134–35
Capital, wealth and, 176–77
Capitalism
  equality and/or freedom under, 138
  fetish of commodity under, 37
  interdependence in, 63
  market function and, 36
  misery and, 36
  private vs. public goods in, 79–80
  profits in, 60–61
  scarcity and, 38
  self-interest in, 36–37
Capitalism and Freedom (Friedman), 130
Carlyle, Thomas, 31
Carnegie-Mellon University, 20
Carter, Jimmy, 100
Carte-blanche reference variables, 49
Ceteris paribus, 52
Checker Taxi Company, 143
Chicago, University of, 133, 144, 147
Chicago taxi monopoly, 142–45
Chicago Yellow Cab Company, 143
China vs. Soviet Union, 136–37
Chinese Revolution, 38
Choice, defined, 57
"Christmas-treeing," 118
Civil Aeronautics Board, 140
Club of Rome, 176, 178
Coase, Ronald H., 147
Coleridge, Samuel Taylor, 31
Colson, Charles, 132
Command system, defined, 59
Commercial banks, 87

Index

Index

Index

Index

Index

Index

Index

About the Author

Leonard Silk is the economic columnist of *The New York Times*, where his pathbreaking column, "The Economic Scene," is a feature of the Times's Business Day section. Mr. Silk has been awarded the Gerald M. Loeb Memorial Award by the University of California for his lifetime contributions to economic journalism, as well as many other prizes. He has received honorary degrees from Duke University and Southeastern Massachusetts University and is a member of the Boards of Visitors of the University of Chicago and the Graduate School of the City University of New York. A former Senior Fellow of the Brookings Institution, he has also taught as Ford Foundation Distinguished Professor and Fairless Lecturer at Carnegie-Mellon University. Mr. Silk took his undergraduate degree at the University of Wisconsin, where he edited the humor magazine, *The Octopus*, and his doctorate degree at Duke University, where he wrote his first book, *Sweden Plans for Better Housing*. His later books include *The Research Revolution, Nixonomics, Ethics and Profits* (with David Vogel), and *The Economists*.